the loose ends became knots

the loose ends became knots

an illness narrative

by

Austin M. Hopkins

library partners press
a digital publishing imprint

ISBN 978-1-61846-048-6

Produced and Distributed By:

Library Partners Press
ZSR Library
Wake Forest University
1834 Wake Forest Road
Winston-Salem, North Carolina 27106

library partners press

a digital publishing imprint

www.librarypartnerspress.org

Manufactured in the United States of America

This book is dedicated to

survivors

of

sexual violence.

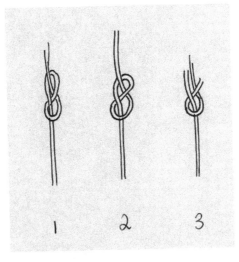

contents

Note.

This project represents my own illness narrative, encompassing a period beginning in August 2012 and continuing through the present day. Explicit descriptions of traumatic events have been selectively omitted in an effort to provide illustrious but conscientious detail. Writing has been a great source of healing for me, and thus, the material included in this project was written over the course of my illness and presents an honest exposé of what I experienced. Entries, unless otherwise noted, are direct excerpts from my journals, poetry, prose, and other writing. This account is comprehensive but not exhaustive; however, I feel that it testifies justly to my illness and to myself.

This project first began as a document I called "the Chronicle," where I documented the detailed events and names (when I had them) of every encounter. This book represents a radical transformation in my ability to tell my story from recounting a list of men that I carried around in my phone to compiling a collection of my intimate thoughts, feelings, fears, and struggles.

I found solace in the French language—it was a mechanism of expressing things that I needed to extract from my mind but wanted to conceal via some mechanism of visual packaging. Many of my first entries and creative works were written in French but have been translated back to English for the ease of sharing my story. However, there are bits and pieces that remain in French, as this is part of how I reminded myself that life could still be beautiful and I wanted to incorporate that very important element into this book.

Where I obtained permission to do so, names of friends remain unchanged. Initials are used for people who I did not wish to name. In other cases, I don't use a name at all.

My hope for this book is that people with similar experiences can hear a narrative that says, "me too." I didn't have many, if any, voices validating the gravity of my experiences in my life during much of my adolescence. To my fellow survivors, both seen and unseen, I hear you. I hear you. I believe you. To those who did not survive, I will work to make the world a more livable, more loving, and safer place.

As I look towards a career in medicine, I have decided that I want to utilize my voice to (1) raise awareness of the pervasive nature of sexual violence within the gay community (as this is the community in which I personally experienced it) and (2) remind the reader, and myself, that there are so many people who suffer from sexual violence who do not have the privilege of or opportunity for speaking publicly without retribution. I want to be a companion, a friend, and a physician for those people.

~Austin M. Hopkins, Fall 2017

part one

the harming

Alice: How long is forever?
White Rabbit: Sometimes, just one second.
-Lewis Carroll, *The Adventures of Alice in Wonderland*

prolegomena

Seven plus eight is 15. Divide 15 by three and you get five. That's the number I decided upon; would you rather prick your finger on a thorn five times or 78 times? It's easier to publicly carry five things than 78. I've sometimes felt like a newly-married couple's car, plastered with toilet paper and dragging empty cans tied to the back bumper behind it as they drive away from the reception. The cans by themselves are light, but in unity, they clatter and clang and they drag along as the car picks up speed, flailing in a wild cacophony generating sparks until their strings are cut. So, yes, it's less taxing, and less invasive, to explain five memories than 78. There are only so many words in a language, anyway. It's easier to describe all that has happened as five distinct episodes with intermittent struggles. It's a way to maintain some façade of dignity in the face of a discriminatory audience. In a story you tell the world, there must be a hero and a villain. It's a socially imposed rule. There must be good and there must be evil. There can't only be grey space; ambiguity doesn't sit well within human nature, which innately seeks resolution, clarity, and closure. As soon as I begin the story, I'm branded with a label of "victim", a tainting, denunciatory overlay that you can't ever completely scrape away.

7

It's easier to say I was sexually assaulted five times. It's not a lie, but it is a fabrication required to talk to most people about why I am who I am at this moment.

Yet it's misleading to say that I carry five or 78 separate entities within me. They are all one; each memory blurs into the next and they create a larger, darker, more magnificent creature that burrows deeply inside me. The creature lives in different places: within the pressure in my chest, the tightening in my throat, the tension of my headaches, the sickness on my stomach, the tremors in my hands, the silence of my voice, the paranoia in my heart. I used to believe that it sought to end me, but in reality, it lives with, rather than against, me. It lives through my memory. When I look at my body, I remember. When I see a man, I see his body as a palate for what could have happened. When I see someone who hurt me, I'm suddenly transported into his respective scene, with a variety of my senses consumed in the flashback.

Regardless of their visceral experience, these things aren't distinct. They aren't simply five; they are much more and much less. They are a tattoo that weaves itself in emphatic patterns across the inside of my body, invisible to the outside world. It will be with me until the end. When I'm asked to talk about it, or when

I want to talk about it, I often don't know where to begin. There were too many beginnings and not enough endings. The threads jump across each other and create knots that I can't seem to untangle in order to distinguish between each microscopic, translucent string. They've melted together into scar tissue that's still raw and bleeding; it's no longer a wound but it's not completely healed, not yet.

a brief lesson in bayesian statistics

<u>Idea:</u> Decisions under Bayesian methodology consider what is "lost" by estimating the true value of a parameter, θ, by a random variable, α.

<u>Definition:</u> A loss function is a real-valued function of two variables, θ & α, denoted by $L(\theta, \alpha)$.

<u>Interpretation:</u> $L(\theta, \alpha)$ is how much is lost if the parameter θ is estimated by α.

<u>Definition:</u> Using the posterior distribution $\pi(\theta \mid X)$, which contains all information on a parameter θ given an observed sample X, we define the expected loss function as $E[L(\theta, \alpha) \mid X) = \int_\Omega L(\theta, \alpha)\pi(\theta \mid X)\, d\theta$.

<u>Interpretation:</u> The expected loss function predicts what we "lose" with any choice of α.

<u>Idea:</u> Chose an estimator α that minimizes the expected loss.

<u>Application:</u> For θ = trauma, chose α = "tell half-truths", where you can release little bits of what information the posterior distribution carries to those you think can handle it, but this may inflate $E[L(\theta, \alpha)$

| X). Chose α = "silence", where no one around you is hurt by what you confess, where $E[L(\theta, \alpha) \mid X)$ is your own composition, there's no product of your pain with their reaction. Or, chose α = "report in full", where $E[L(\theta, \alpha) \mid X)$ is your dignity, at best. Or maybe you'll chose α = "*l'appel du vide*", where $E[L(\theta, \alpha) \mid X)$ is either infinitely maximized or minimized, depending on your perspective. The extent of how large, threatening, complicated, monstrous, or simple $E[L(\theta, \alpha) \mid X)$ can be all depends on your choice of α.

the t word

What is it, really? Is it something that leaves physical scars that you must try to hide? Is it something that destroys your faith and trust in yourself? Is it something that leaves you feeling numb, or in denial that it happened? Is it something that you feel as though you can't talk about it in fear of dismissal or judgment? Is it something that leads to cyclical episodes in which you witness your consciousness separate from your physical body, involuntarily relinquishing control of what happens to or with your body? Is it something that you can't emotionally access? Is it something that you think about almost every day in an attempt to parameterize its enormity to be able to have something tangible upon which to lean? Is it something that you once held yourself accountable for and hated yourself for having had it happen to you? Is it something that happened not of your own volition that tries its best to threaten your ability to be whole, to be free?

flashback: the white house

I most vividly remember the nights we sat on your
couch, watching 90's BBC specials and the London
Olympics, and the nights speeding through dark, oak
tree-lined downtown streets in your dark blue BMW
with the windows down; the wind ripping around my
head and your hand on my inner thigh, I felt invincible
and finally, as if it was okay to be gay. This was a
pleasure that I had forbidden myself until I met you.
But I also remember the night I sobbed on my way
home, blasting Passion Pit's *Gossamer* from the car
speakers, the thudding base subtly overpowering the
pain trying to crack open my chest. I remember still
responding to your texts as I drove, trying to get
home before my mom called the person who I said I
was with after I'd massively broken my curfew, which
would have revealed that I was not where I'd told my
parents I was. I remember what you took from me,
that which I never got back.

30 august 2012

These past two weeks haven't been good to me;
they've been two weeks of decline into a place where I
don't see a way out. But today I felt alive for the first
time in a while. I was in the pool. It's just me and the
water. I swim lap after lap, faster and faster until every
fiber of my body aches. It's here where I can justly
hurt and push harder and struggle to breathe and ache
and it's okay because there is a physical source to my
struggle: the water. I can move it and push it and it
doesn't fight back, and the coolness is soothing to my
skin. It's not my head, or my heart, that I have to
battle. It's chlorinated water; something I know how
to control and manipulate and something that absorbs
my outburst with love.

15 october 2012

I hadn't eaten in over 24 hours and I felt undamaged.
Last night at the frat party I had 12 cups of punch
(with questionable amounts of everclear and vodka and
who knows what else) and felt fine. But what hurts the
most is how I'm being pushed away by the people I
thought would still want me around. I look into their
eyes, and I can't figure out what I've done to deserve
abandonment. I know I'm a poor friend, but you have
to understand how fucking hard I'm fighting at the
moment. So yeah, I won't always act normally or nice
or pleasant or whatever the hell you want from me. I'm
tired of dealing with your bullshit and I can't handle it
right now. It's dramatic, but I fear that I am on the
verge of the abyss. I have to wait a few weeks to go get
help. Give me some fucking credit.

flashback: a place i used to love

You told me not to worry, it wouldn't hurt for long.
You didn't even take off your shirt as you pushed deep
into me before I had the chance to respond. I felt
something begin to rise throughout my body,
culminating in a hollow, pulsing pressure in the base of
my throat. My mouth hung open and I kissed you
robotically but I wasn't in control of what my body
was doing, or where we were heading; I was subject to
a compulsive driving force that didn't respect what I
wanted and then suddenly, you let it out inside of me
and I realized with sickening clarity that what was
now inside should have been elsewhere. You left me on
the bed, saying that it was fine and that I had nothing
to worry about, but I couldn't reverse the explosion
and now the risk was brewing and I couldn't get it out.

My consciousness fled outside of my body and I was
absent to the world around me until three months
later, when the risk was nulled by the phone call I
made after class to the woman who read the results in
a blasé tone, as if they didn't control the direction of
my future.

I was terrified that it was going to end me; that I was
going to succumb to you. I won't forget the fear you

implanted in me, figuratively and literally. It was a
sticky, nauseating fear that stuck itself in my throat
and it choked me, it gagged me, it made me want to
vomit out my insides, and to burn them, to kill
whatever was living in me.

an exchange

The scene opens on a sunlit room; two walls are lined with bookshelves full of bulky psychology texts and trinkets collected from twenty years of holidays abroad. Two chairs sit across from a yellow, sagging sofa. A middle-aged man in black, rectangular Ray-Ban glasses works at the computer on the dark, wooden desk that sits in the corner. A young, slim woman in a bright pink blouse and black pants sits in the left chair. A young boy sits on the far corner of the sofa; he's thin, pale, and his fingers tap out a repetitive pattern on his pant leg. The man pretends to work at the computer but is clearly attentive to the conversation.

INTERN: Is this your first time at the University Counseling Center?

BOY: Yes, yes it is.

INTERN: Okay. Thank you for coming in today. Can you tell me what brings you in?

BOY: Well, I think I'm depressed. I can't seem to get out of this funk. I feel listless and heavy, as if there's a cloud that's sunk into my head and I can't clear it. I know that depression runs in my family, so I'm not surprised that I feel this way. I've been trying to exercise, eat well, and get regular sleep but it's not helping. I know that drinking has probably made it worse. I also, um, I was with someone recently and it didn't go well. I can't stop thinking about it; I feel guilty and ashamed and I can't sleep through the night because I feel so afraid.

INTERN: What do you mean?

BOY: He didn't treat me very well and it feels like he took advantage of me. It makes me feel bad, and I don't know what to do. I don't know his name and I don't know if he actually hurt me or if I just didn't enjoy it. I don't know what to do.

INTERN: What do you mean, you don't know what to do?

BOY: I can't remember exactly what happened, and maybe it was my fault, maybe I'm remembering things wrong.

INTERN: Are you sure?

BOY: I don't know.

INTERN: Well, what you're saying doesn't make much sense. You expressed that you're feeling depressed but you're doing things to address it, and you said that this intimate encounter could be just a bad experience. It just seems a little hypocritical to me, because you seem to know what's wrong so you should know how best to address it yourself.

BOY: Oh.

The appointment ends a bit later, the boy having said very little after the first exchange. The director only made eye contact with the boy and spoke his first word, "Thanks", when the boy got up to leave. The boy doesn't go back. Not after the next time it happens, or the next, or the one after that.

flashback: corner of fourth street.

With your small, stubby hand on my head, you pressed my head into the itchy beige carpet and I saw spots of lights in my vision where they weren't supposed to exist. Your force hit me deeply, serving as unrelenting evidence that I was a warm, malleable mannequin meant to fulfil your carnal agenda. You'd pushed me to the floor as if I was unfit for the bed; as I lay on my stomach, the weight of your writhing body grinding me into the carpet, I stared at the dirt and dust that had collected in the corners beneath your bed. I never spent as much time staring at dust bunnies as I did that night. You showed me the door after an eternity. I left with a rash on my face, a hollowness in my abdomen, a soreness in my core and a tightness in my muscles that kept me company as I drove back to campus and walked to my dorm in the cold, March rain.

flashback: suburbia

You had me pinned down and your weight was suffocating. Even if I'd found a way to move, I don't know what I would have done. You outweighed me by at least a hundred pounds; I couldn't breathe, I couldn't move, I couldn't obey the screaming voice in my head that told me to get away, that this man wanted to hurt me. I knew I needed to leave but I couldn't. This was the first time that I can remember thinking *I might die tonight, this man might kill me.* But once again I was physically unable to speak, to scream, or to even turn over. It was hard enough to breathe. When you finished and went to the bathroom to showed off, I managed to silently grab my clothes and keys and ran out of the small house, the one you said was your grandmother's and I got in my car and drove furiously away. My heart raced and I was afraid to look behind me in case I saw you run out of the house towards your car. I didn't know where I was going or where I was, really, but I knew where I was not. I didn't cry, or speak, or do anything on the drive back to school except stare at the empty highway. I didn't sleep that night. But I managed to go to class in the morning, I always did.

the others (15 may 2013)

"Will you take your brother to swim practice? I have to run to the grocery store and the dry cleaners on my way home and won't be back in time to take him."

Thank god. I'm grateful for a moment to be alone this afternoon, after having missed my call-in window on Monday due to a final exam. The anxiety of envisioning myself having to call in my mother's presence finally lifts, allowing me to focus on the deeper anxiety of what I'd be calling for. I told my brother I'd be taking him to the pool in five minutes, and as he was packing his swim bag I checked my wallet to make sure the card was inside. It was still there, smirking with condescension, and I pulled it out to feel it in my hands for tangible proof that it existed. We drove in the company of one of my mix CD's; no words were exchanged between the two of us except for "Call when you're out. Have fun, I love you" and "I love you too". Nothing would be remembered as peculiar except for in my own retrospect, where I could feel the enormous pressure threatening to rip open my throat and reveal itself to everyone in the parking lot. I drove to the furthest space from the club entrance and parked. Three minutes. I checked various social media apps absentmindedly, trying to fill the time with something mind-numbing. My mind was counting seconds, milliseconds, and time slowed, almost to a stop.

3:44. I took out the card.

3:45. I dialed the number I had dialed before, except for this time, I could not be sure of the response that I was to receive. My heart pounded in synch with my finger's light taps on my phone, and my eyes lost focus of the cars in front of me as I held the phone to my right ear. My heartbeat threatens to bust my ear drums, I can barely hear the dial tone. Three rings, and she picked up.

How may I help you?

I'm calling for test results.

Date of birth? Last name?

We both sat in silence. It was too long, my mouth began to form the sob—

Your results for gonorrhea and syphilis are negative.

I choked, I exhaled, but there was still a threat—

And the others?

She asked me to hold, that she needed to confirm something. The following silence swallowed me into its expanse, threatening me with impending damnation. My mouth formed the O of an impending scream, a sob, or anything that would let the monster out—

Your Hepatitis results are negative and your HIV results are negative.

My chest opened up, and something dark and electric and spiny fled into the nearby woods. My face was dry; relief streamed out as invisible pressure jets from my eye sockets. I put my car into drive and went home to help my mother make dinner.

talking to myself (26 august 2013)

The words you read, the ones you wrote long ago

Can you remember why you wrote them?

Can you remember?

Did you feel that sadness you described, or was that feeling something else?

Flashes of things that happened come suddenly and then they go

Just like him, he came and now you want him to go

The sun shines bright and cold but you hide inside

Writing about things that have no other place to go

Can you separate the smeared blobs of colors on your palette?

Where are places for all the memories to go?

Can you find a place for him to go, a place not scripted by the endless scarring?

Relief is what you crave and regret erects the barricade around your hell

In and out, in and out, you straddle a twilight zone

But still you have no safe place, no retreat, no hiding
place to go

To scatter the pieces, to draw the map of where
insidious river currents flow

This sickness has a name, it has a face and a shape

And now it conforms to the volume of your mind

And you leave it with no place to go

Because you have no other place to go

a bbc special

On the dry, sun-blazed savannah, the lioness patiently watches her prey, flicking a fly away when it ventures too close to her warm body as she crouches on her haunches, camouflaged seamlessly within the tall, golden grass. Her eyes blink and narrow, tracing the gentle movements of the gazelle grazing just a few feet away. The lioness is patient, she won't strike until she's ready, until the prey is perfectly vulnerable, unaware, and unable to escape or defend itself. The lioness waits. If you listen closely, you can hear the slightest purr.

flashback: the roommate

You watched me revolve in a kaleidoscope called melancholia, rearranging pieces and people and places, trying to make something I could hold onto during the semester from hell. You watched me devolve into something unreachable, something toxic. You watched me while I slept, while I worked, while I retreated into the depths of my own guilt. You judged me and you provoked me to pull away from the people who love(d) me. I followed you into the dark corner of cynicism where nothing in the world could be celebrated. I don't think I realized how closely I trailed you into that dark place; I didn't realize I was even there until I came out of it. When I went to the bottle to find something to fill the role of a savior, you watched me carefully. You watched me disintegrate into a muddled being, where couldn't exactly distinguish reality from hallucinations. I passed out in my bed during the movie we were watching on the last day of class and when I woke up you were on top of me, doing the things you'd later admit to having fantasized about, and I felt something implode and felt the torrent of falling into a deeper crevice, losing the shred of resolve I'd held onto that spring.

I got away as soon as I could, but you were still there when I looked behind my back. You followed me all summer, trying to convince me that what you did wasn't what I thought it was. I believed you briefly, I even believed for a short time that it was my fault. But now I see it for what it was, and I see you for what you were. You're concretely part of my memories of sophomore year, of Wake Forest, of sex, of tall blonde men, of theater, of English majors, of Fireball Whisky and *American Hustle*, the movie we were watching when I fell backwards onto my bed in a drunken stupor.

30 may 2014

So yes, this isn't how I want to die. But isn't death truly honest, is it not what will set me free?

this is your life (june 2014)

But you shove it to the back of your throat

You never thought this would be your life
But this is your life
Eyes closed, it's not there if you can't see it

Wishing on every star, every random chance
Praying to something greater that it all would fade
away
But well-wishes are interrupted by intuitive sense
The potency, the toxicity, the guilt
Three beggars in a self-consuming inferno
Accompanists down a dimming path
Into the End.

the room with the red carpet: un roman à clef (part one)

At the end of freshman year, the boy received an email explaining that his roommate for the fall semester had dropped out and he needed to find someone else share his double room. The boy began thinking of the few male classmates he knew, trying to identify someone who might make a good roommate. Then he thought of S, the tall, quiet lanky blonde he met recently through a group of friends. S was aloof but the boy admired his punk-rock vibe. The boy didn't know much about him but had mutual friends. Thus, S couldn't be too bad. When he asked S to room with him, S said *yes, that'd be cool.*

The boy moved in early to participate as a student leader for a first-year pre-orientation program. The boy's room was in the home across the road from campus was tiny: a tiny double room in half of a converted garage. There was barely room to de-bunk the single beds. The beds were almost touching, parallel to each other. The room had deep burgundy red carpet, the kind that immediately looks dirty again after each cleaning. The boy began to plaster his side of the room with notecards of quotes and posters to hide the barren white walls. It felt like an incubator-turned prison, that little room. The boy rarely his room that year. He didn't know, nor want to know, the other people in the house. That room was a prison, but sometimes one that was chosen because it was safe. Sometimes it was a safe prison. Sometimes.

The first night, S hadn't moved in yet. The boy's boyfriend, L, was visiting for the night from Raleigh, and they slept together in the tiny single bed. The next day, S moved in while the pair were out for the day. He was quiet, not saying much when the boy introduced himself and L. Maybe it was awkward for S as well. The boy hadn't thought of that. Over the next few weeks, S and the boy began developing a deeper friendship. They laughed together at night, watching Netflix and bonding over the daily experience of being branded with "other-ness" at a highly conservative and Greek-life-centered university. The boy believed that S was, at the very least, a confidante in the making.

As the weeks passed, the boy began to become uncomfortable in his relationship with L, and as time passed, the tension from distance inserted in a fairly new relationship grew stronger. The boy eventually cheated on L with a random guy he met off of Grindr. They met at an apartment that this guy was caring for while a friend was out of town. Regret filled him as soon as he sat down on the couch, but he couldn't find the will to move or to stop anything that happened. When he came home, he told S what he had done and pretended to cry into S's shoulder as S tried to comfort him in his awkward, silent way. He thought that S was someone who would understand and console him without expressing harsh, punitive judgment.

He doesn't remember exactly what S said once he admitted that he had cheated on L. It wasn't completely accepting, but was a slightly vicious undertone overlaid by a supportive hug. Something like that.

As the fall semester progressed, the boy suffered from what he would later christen as 'the episodes'. He fell into the cycles of Grindr binges, and in these cycles, he lost the ability to speak about what was happening. He had no control over the progression of events; he couldn't say 'stop', he couldn't say 'no', he couldn't say anything at all. He'd disappear after spending hours in bed on his phone to come back late in the night, most likely smelling strongly and noticeably of sex. He tried to talk about it with friends, but they didn't quite understand what he was trying to say. Not even the boy knew what he meant. He tried to frame the sexual encounters as an act of rebellious deviance that happened to leave him feeling used and shitty, if not physically hurt. During one of these cycles the boy went to an apartment that he'd never been to before. This was nothing unusual. The boy often showed up timidly outside apartment doors and at unfamiliar, unlit houses. He trusted that the person on the other side of the Grindr connection was honest because that's all he could do. This night, the person that opened the door was not someone new, but rather the first person who hurt him. The first guy who'd inserted his rough, callous fingers into a tight place without consent or any lubricant. The boy still can feel the pain. He still can't let anyone, not even people he trusts, traverse this territory without his heart racing and his breath falling under a heavy weight. When the door opened, the boy's breath fell away and he felt his legs carry him breathlessly inside. The fear in his chest was painful, expanding past the physical boundaries of ribs and skin. The man said it was nice to see him again, did the boy like his new place? The boy nodded and smiled, as the cycle commanded how the boy's body moved and responded, no matter what the boy's conscience screamed from within the sealed-off chamber of rational thinking somewhere in his brain. But then there was a rare moment of freedom. While the man went to the bathroom, the boy bolted. He ran out of the apartment and ran up the street back to his parked car, looking behind him every so often, afraid that he'd see the man watching him go. The man messaged him on Grindr, asking if he'd scared the boy away. Then the man blocked the boy. The boy thinks his name is Robert. But there's no clear face attached to these memories, not any longer.

There was nowhere else in town to go on a Tuesday night in October, so the boy went back to school, feeling fragile and frightfully aware of how he was still afraid. He went to his friends' suite on campus, looking for Meredith, who he hoped wouldn't judge him if he confided in her. He sat in her room and talked, and she listened. She was with him in a way that no other person had been before; he felt safe, sitting on her bed holding her hand in silence.

Then S arrived. He'd been walking around campus, like he usually did at night, thinking. He was upset that the boy had silently gone off into the night. S was trying to figure out what to do, what to say, to mitigate the anger and frustration and judgment writhing inside of him. When he stormed into the suite he went into the room where the boy and Meredith were and exploded. He yelled at both of them, calling them stupid for to romanticizing and condoning promiscuous sexual encounters. He called them irresponsible and he continued on, his words flying wildly like shrapnel. The boy was afraid, again. The power of the emotions being thrown at him were frightening, revealing a wealth of pent-up frustration inside of S that had been brewing for months. Trying to explain what had happened had no effect on S. The memories grow dim for the boy after this, he's not sure of how the situation deflated.

But the boy and S eventually improvised peace, although the memory of S's outburst remained ablaze within the boy's mind. The fear he felt in the presence of S was surprising, unsettling, and unnerving. The reality that there was much more beneath the surface; the boy didn't know the depth of the person who slept so close to him. The beds in the tiny room had been rearranged into a U formation, with S at the far end. He remembers spending many sleepless nights in this formation. The boy didn't sleep well that year, for a variety of reasons: being closeted, being overwhelmed with school, suffering from untreated depression and trying to survive the cycles that broke him down and left feeling defeated. He started to think about death often, what it would feel like, how it could happen, what it would mean if it were to happen soon. Nothing serious and no formal contemplation or planning. Just thoughts.

The boy would sometimes wake up to find S still awake late at night, or technically, early morning. Even without his glasses, he could see S watching him. He let these observations fall away at the time. He took it as a sign of compassion and care that S watched him while he slept. In retrospect, he feels afraid that S watched him every night. What was he thinking as he watched? What thoughts repeated themselves over and over cyclically while the boy slept?

The next months were hard for the boy. The spring semester classes were uninteresting and challenging, and his composure was slipping away. He felt desperate and broken. He lashed out at his family, his friends, his acquaintances. He let his commitments fall away. He would stop talking for days at a time, after S would say something hurtful or judgmental. The best way to solve these problems was to ignore them, or at least that's how the boy survived. He didn't manage, he survived. That's all he could do.

When the boy and S were on speaking terms, they would sometimes talk late at night about being at Wake Forest and about the people they knew and interacted with and felt oppressed by. Retrospect makes this fact clear: S tried to make the boy hate everyone on the outside of that room. The girls he spent most of his time took advantage of him and didn't reciprocate his emotional investment. His friends in his classes (especially the ones in sororities) were fake and catty and made the boy a different person who was to be despised. S said that these people

were using the boy, exploiting him, that he needed to
let them go. Stay in on a Friday night instead of going
out and becoming too drunk, sleeping on toilets and
vomiting up burning mucous remains of punch and
shots. The boy began to believe S, overlaying S's
suggestions and commentary on the relationships that
were already strained. He decided to go abroad in the
fall to get away from everything, as he hated Wake
Forest and everyone there. He hated his life.

The cycles continued, and the boy felt tarnished and
out of control. But the cycles were what sustained him,
as each time he was fucked, he finally felt alive. The
pain of each thrust and the feeling of cum splattering
on his torso and his face were sensations that made
him feel as though his conscious self and his body were
temporarily united. At all other times, he felt empty, a
passive voyeur to a slowly disintegrating ghost. Fear
and physical pain were the uniting factors for moments
when he felt alive. Everything else felt dead.

The end of the semester had arrived. Refuge in a
semester abroad was only a summer away. On the last
day of classes the boy decided to drink away the fear of
failing his exams, to find refuge in nothingness. The
boy put on *American Hustle* on the television above his
bed and he drank Fireball Whisky from the bottle,
losing himself in the warmth of the burn as it fell down

his throat. Sips turned into gulps that turned into an empty bottle laying on the desk. S was there, too, watching. Watching what, the boy can't remember. The boy doesn't remember the end of the movie, just that he laughed like he hadn't all semester, this level of intoxication was liberating. The emptiness and swirling fluids in his head made him need to lie down, and he did. In his bed, facing the window and the door. It was semi-dark, some light falling in from the windows facing the road as he felt his eyes close and the heaviness of drunken slumber fall over him.

He woke up some time later in total darkness and to the comforting warmth of a body; S was in his single bed behind him. To have anyone hold the boy felt okay, it temporarily appeased the toxicity festering inside the boy's chest. But the boy knew that S shouldn't be in his bed; he didn't want this to happen, this was strange. S was only in his white, semi-transparent spandex underwear. Poking through the rocking delirium of a dangerous level of intoxication, the boy felt the penis against his back as S pressed against him. This delirium was dissociative, the boy's conscious self was meters away in the sticky air watching what was happening to his drunken body. The physical sensations registered softly, not interrupting the reverie of dissociation. The boy felt a growing hardness against his back, a flaccid penis growing stronger. The boy closed his eyes, his body preparing for yet another cycle. Then somehow the boy's hand was being pulled to S's underwear, even though the boy's conscious self was screaming *no, no, no! Don't do this! Stop it--you're too drunk and this is bad.* But then S's grip tightened, and his hand peeled off his underwear, releasing its captive member. Then S's hand found the boy's own waistline, the cold boniness of his touch electrifying and paralyzing. He pulled down the boy's pants and yanked off his shirt. The boy was silent, as always, even though the screaming and yelling and miserable wailing inside his head was deafening. *Close your eyes,* the boy thought, *and maybe this won't be real.* Then he was rolled on his back and then S was on top of him, the slimy snake of a tongue invading his mouth. The kissing didn't stop when the boy didn't kiss back. The bony hand was groping the boy's genitals, creating a betraying physiological response that the boy condemned as what had to be a sickening joke. The boy doesn't know how long this lasted. Then S whispered *I want to fuck you, I want to fuck you, you want me to fuck you* as he began to dry hump the boy, pressing his hardness against the boy's body, coming close to the fantasy's epitome. The boy was screaming inside, *run away run away fuck you run away don't do this to me don't do this to me I want to die.* A few more moments and then S's face moved away and his hands reached down to push through the last layer

of interference between his cock and the sacred place
he wanted to fuck but at this last moment, something
analogous to lightning struck in the boy's mind. By
what god it came from, he doesn't know. The
momentum rolled him out of bed on the burgundy-
carpeted floor, where he pulled on clothes and ran
outside. He still was too drunk to be able to properly
run away, to think about driving, too drunk to be able
to even cross the street. He tried calling people, but no
one would answer at 3 am. No one was awake, not
now, he was on his own. S came outside, crying, saying
he was sorry, *this wasn't how I wanted it to happen. This
is not how I imagined it happening.* Pre-meditation
admitted, who knows what encompassed the full
fantasy. The boy broke. He couldn't find another place
to go but back to that room, that bed, where he fell
asleep or he passed out, the boy can't tell a difference.

What other choice did the boy have but to move along
with the current of the flood? Exams were looming,
but the boy wilted under the pressure to achieve
perfection for his future medical school applications.
Unable to study at all, he saw a movie with Meredith,
who called him as soon as she woke up and saw his
missed calls; she listened and heard him once again and
he felt love for the first time in a long time. They saw
Nymphomaniac, a movie whose message was too
applicable to be emotionally accessible for the boy to

digest at that moment in time. As time passed, though, the film would come to validate him for feeling torn, broken, hurt; feelings that barely encapsulate the pain that prickled with each inhale and exhale. A poisonous gas was trapped inside the constraints of his ribcage, filling his lungs with a permeable toxicity that swam around his circulation and then his body felt heavy with waterlogged sand.

The first exams came and went. The boy was able to survive, to take them, to turn something in. He ignored S. Ignoring his reality was the only way to survive, to make it to the next week when he could escape the room with red carpet and peeling white walls by going home for the summer. *Just hang in there,* he thought over and over, *you can make it. Just hang in there.*

On Saturday night, he fell asleep to the silent tension that filled the room when he and S were present. It was late and he fell asleep quickly to the sweet, relieving oblivion that was sleep.

A blaring noise awoke the boy. His lamp was still on, meaning S had not yet gone to bed. The room was blurry, his glasses were on the table. S stood in the doorway, heaving, crying, screaming unintelligibly.

The boy saw the blood spouting from S's face and he instantly awoke.

Nothing contained within the next nine hours felt real: calling the police, washing S off in the bathroom, talking to the police about the armed robbery that had occurred right outside their bedroom, driving to the hospital in the early morning, waiting while the physician tied the stitches, waiting for S's mother to arrive. He could barely summon energy to find help for S, to get the blood out of the carpet, to stay awake in the waiting room of the emergency department.

The last exam came and went and then he went home where he collapsed into himself, where no one could touch him. He found a place where he could dissolve himself into oblivion.

At home, the events of early May felt distant, surreal, as if they hadn't happened anywhere outside of the boy's imagination. He dealt with the residual physical side effects of the semester: crippling depression, constant tension headaches, exhaustion he could never shake. He lived day by day, and that was it. He went to visit his friends in Winston one Saturday, looking forward to a housewarming party for his friends' new off-campus home. He missed them, he missed the liberty of being able to be himself authentically. Being at home was hard because he was closeted: his sexuality, his experiences, his needs, they were all hidden away in the darkest corner of himself. Going to his friends for a night promised freedom and a reason to smile.

The night of the party, as he was beginning to become very drunk, the door to the living room opened and S walked in. They made eye contact, and the boy felt something crumple inside him and fall away. His lungs collapsed, his heart shriveled in upon itself, he felt his throat constrict. How the hell was he here? Why was he here? Why? The girls he was visiting knew a limited extent of what had happened. But S was still invited, and he still came.

The boy proceeded to drink more, to rudimentarily placate the hole that was opening in his chest. He didn't sleep that night, afraid that someone would burst through the door to attack him on the pull-out sofa in the living room. He was very afraid.

For the Fourth of July, the boy went back to visit the girls. He hoped that S wouldn't show up, that last time was weird enough and the boy hoped he would stay away.

But he didn't. And the boy was incredibly drunk for most of the weekend to deal with the pain. To deal with the anger and fear and sadness all bundled within his mind.

Meredith invited her friend from home, an attractive guy whose confidence and exuberance was intoxicating. In his drunken state, the boy began to be infatuated with this guy, hoping to be fucked hard and to feel physical pain to viscerally redistribute the immensity of what was within him—and to put a more beautiful face to his pain.

The first night his efforts were futile. He tried sleeping alone but the fear and panic and emotion was overwhelming. S came downstairs from where he was sleeping and told the boy to come upstairs, to sleep with him. The boy followed S into an empty bed, just big enough for two. The boy began to talk, telling about futile romances and the hardships of the summer. The boy apologized for something, he can't remember what. He felt bad for what he felt, and somehow an apology slipped out, casting all the blame for everything that had happened upon the boy himself.

The next day was spent in a semi-conscious drunken haze, as the boy kept drinking to put off the hangover and reality and the feelings that were placated by intoxication. S was in his periphery; always close, but not always close enough to have to talk to. The boy ignored him, ashamed of what had happened the night before. *Ignore it so it isn't real,* the boy's insides said. *Pretend it didn't happen. It didn't have to happen if you don't want it to.*

That night the boy kissed Meredith's friend. They slept together on the pull-out bed and the boy's body kept pushing him closer, trying to initiate a cycle to feel the pain he needed to feel. S had long since retreated to mope upstairs, knowing very well was going on. The boy left early the next morning, saying goodbye to only the people who got up as early as he did.

24 july 2015

Where I am: Montlawn Memorial Park, Raleigh, NC
What I feel: the warmth of the setting July sun, the
itchy green blades of grass, the callous grains of dirt I
rub between my fingers, my hand on the cold, grey
plaque in the ground in front of me
What I hear: the passing of rush hour traffic on the
interstate, the sounds of geese down at the large
fountain, my voice saying *What happened, Grandma,
what happened, how did it all go wrong?*

aperture (3 august 2014)

I felt guilty after it happened. Did I really have the
right to shatter all my mother's dreams of who I would
be? Her vision of me being devoted to a church, to her
god: gone. Her vision of being at my wedding to a
beautiful woman: gone. Her vision of helping to care
for her biological grandchildren: gone. Her vision of
who she wanted me to be, what she'd worked so hard
for in raising me for the last 20 years: gone. Who was I
to take all that away from her? It was an argument
that took an unexpected, revelatory turn. I didn't know
I was going to share those things. I didn't realize what
I was doing until they fell out of my mouth. But once
they had, I could never take them back. I tried to feel
proud, to feel relieved, to feel as if I'd not just crushed
my mother, who was throwing up in the bathroom of
our hotel room. The friends that I called while sitting
out in the hotel garden responded with exuberant
congratulations and genuine excitement for "the brave
thing" I'd done. But I couldn't feel proud. I was scared
of what would happen when I went back—had I just
compromised the love from my family? I sat in the
garden for hours, until my dad came to find me to
inform me that Mom was really sick. We ended our
vacation early, and I knew that what I had done was
not simply just coming out.

15 august 2014

The first day I was able to cry since 10 October, 2009.

My mother sent me to a therapist of her choosing, one with a Christianity-steeped practice, but I made sure that the first words that came out of my mouth were to defend myself, to push back before anything could come at me. I told him that I would talk, but I did not want to hear anything about god or Jesus or anything of that nature. I was surprised--he complied.

the t word, again (22 august 2014)

The therapist introduced the four-letter acronym that would become my diagnosis. I didn't believe him. I didn't think what had happened was 'bad enough'. I felt like there was something else, something darker and innately crueler that had to happen to me before I could claim that label. I was not 'ruined' enough, I reasoned. My physical flesh was still intact, I'd not taken a gun to my temple, I hadn't found myself in the emergency room after any of these events, so there was still something worse that could happen to me. If that thing ever happened, then I could claim these things. Then I could reconsider.

written in the margin of my journal (5 september 2014)

"You're not a bad person for the ways you tried to kill your sadness. You're just human, and being human means you need to survive and you do so whichever way you deem fit, fuck everyone else."   -Unknown

wisdom from a friend

"Pushing against something means leaning into it. You thought you were resisting, but you were falling the whole time." –Taylor

the mother figure

"I first met Austin during the London Orientations for his Study Abroad experience at Queen Mary University of London. It was after Austin moved in to the dorm at Queen Mary I first heard from one of my staff that Austin had requested to meet with us to discuss the situation there. Austin had chatted with one of my staff who felt this young man was experiencing a very severe crisis and I was brought into the equation. I noticed immediately that Austin was suffering considerably and needed immediate help. After many years of working with students, I have experienced when students are truly suffering and Austin was incredibly fragile at that point. I immediately recommended that he had an appointment with my own GP and I also made an appointment with a psychologist with whom I have worked with for many years. Between the two professionals they helped Austin get through the crisis he was experiencing.

When Students come to us staff and feel able to elaborate on how they are feeling always puts us in a privileged position. I am not an expert in the health area but I have had so many experiences that I feel I am able to slot into a students life as their confidante. Austin seemed so fragile that I wanted to make sure he felt he had the support he deserved to face life here in London. My feelings towards Austin was almost maternal in a very strange way and I just wanted to build his confidence and to make him like himself again.

One of the questions I have been asked is what was the challenge I faced. I suppose the challenge was to help this young man feel his self-worth and to help him understand how his loved ones could help him in the healing process. His biggest challenge was his own family and I wanted to help bridge that for both parties to heal and to help each other accept different outlooks in life. When I am dealing with extremely unhappy students and students with deep anxiety issues, my one fear is that they experience harmful thoughts. It makes me very nervous and as I am not the health expert, I tend to act incredibly swiftly to involve experts. Initially, I felt Austin was in a very vulnerable state and wanted my staff to keep an eye on him at all times.

As for Austin's future, well, I think he grew into a confidant young man whilst being out of his own country and the separation from his family may have helped all parties to accept the person he is. I have heard from Austin a few times where he has spoken of his self-growth in London which will help him throughout his life. He recognised his lows and worked himself out of that with help from professionals. I know Austin will remember that for the rest of his life and hope it will be a good sounding board for when life throws difficult times at him in the future. Austin must always remember his self-worth, to love himself and with that he will be able to help others."

Austin, this was written from my heart. I hope it helps but that is exactly how I felt when I first met you.

Good luck with everything. I know you will be a successful young man in the field of medicine.

-Lynne

sanctum: un roman à clef (october 2014)

The clouds hung heavily in the sky, grey blankets that
obscured the sun's warmth from reaching the damp
Earth. *This is why people think England is dreary*, he
thought, sitting in the front table of the coffee shop.
The window was cold, the bustling of students moving
from module to module filled the space with a
reverberating, rhythmic chatter. The bricks of the
courtyard shone with remnants of the morning's
drizzle, and the gleam caught the boy's eye as he let
his gaze wander from a steady focus. The time between
modules was expansive and monotonous; his mind fell
into grey doldrums as he sat alone in various places.
The doldrums flirted with his consciousness tirelessly,
they were where his accent gave him away as being a
fraud, an educational tourist at a prized institution for
the full-time students enrolled there. They were at the
school where he fell apart during the first week, letting
endless rivers of tears erupted over phone calls home.
Let me come home, he pleaded, *this was a mistake.* That
plea was never answered, but he did move across the
city into a warm, white row house in Notting Hill
among the city's wealthiest addresses. He felt at home
with housemates he called friends, in a house that he
loved. But at school he was a transitory presence, as if
it were almost wrong that he even be there. He kept to

himself, devoting himself to studying and writing to fill the time. In Arts Two, he tried to stay focused while the hordes of students gossiped and giggled before, during, and after lecture. In the coffee shop with harsh, lime green walls, he usually sat sipping an overly-expensive Americano. He sat attempting to be studious in the quiet upper floors of the library, or downstairs among the mingling students, who chattered about failed tests and essay ideas and of last night's debacle at Ministry of Sound in Elephant & Castle where they snorted questionable lines of what was rumored to be coke. Every day in the dining hall, he sat with a book in his hand as he ate lunch alone.

Reviewing formulas and proofs and highlighting important passages in library books only filled a finite number of minutes; the problem sets and readings couldn't stretch themselves wide enough to cover the daily expanse of undirected time. The remainder became quiet solitude, in this place or that one. The boy became familiar with many of the pupils in his lectures, listening to their stories and concerns and queries among the small circles of friends that formed in the public areas of the school. He watched the other Americans lead their lives at school, but he pretended to be engrossed in the blurring pages of the book he happened to be holding when they drew close. He walked quickly between buildings, eyes boring into the screen of his phone as he pretended that it wasn't wifi-dependent. Every minute was a deliberate attempt to be invisible. Even though his clothes were slightly too American, his backpack too, hopefully no one would notice if he didn't speak. Silence was comforting after the first few weeks. It made living a little easier if he didn't have to suppress the afflictions coating his insides. The pin pricks that stuck him with every word he said in forced conversations lost their pain when he chose silence instead.

That day, as he sat watching people walk outside the window, his phone kept lighting up with messages. A man named M, an East Londoner. A connection made on Grindr, where the boy's profile indicated he was an American student here in London, looking to meet new guys. M's picture showcased a full, dark brown beard punctuated by blazing green eyes. His chest was hairy, muscular, and well-defined. Every time a new message appeared, it was this image that came to the boy's mind. Every nuanced flirtation, every blunt question, every minute of that day spent planning the evening's date. The nerves that spun in a whirlpool in the boy's stomach created a familiar tension. The knowledge that this man may not be real, or may be something unfathomable, that knowledge led the flurries that blossomed in his stomach to travel up and down his body, his mind growing numb.

As the last lecture ended, the students packed their things and headed towards the Mile End Tube station. Darkness had fallen by 16:30. The boy deviated from his usual path to the Underground and instead found a seat at the bus stop on the bridge over the canal. He kept checking his phone for the screenshot of the route. He waited silently, trying to shove his nerves deeper into his torso, somewhere between his lungs and his ribcage. The mothers, the students, the workers standing with him were just as silent, honoring British custom. Don't look around, don't question, don't let your eyes betray your curiosity or your truth.

The bus arrived and the boy scanned his Oyster card and chose a window seat on the nearly empty bus. He began counting the stops, waiting for the J stop somewhere further north towards the border with Hackney. The bus jostled through damp, dark streets lined by sagging brick buildings; the small windows with blue and grey shutters frowned at passerby. The bus continued through the streets lined by Punjabi take-away restaurants, overflowing convenience marts, and other small boutiques whose lights shown feebly through the mist that would settle with dusk. At the J stop, the boy disembarked and tried to not let his fear paint itself on his face. This was real now, his meeting a stranger in the part of the city to which he'd never been. He followed the route illuminated on his phone, up off the high street and towards the canal, where stout apartment buildings were crowded together around fenced-in squares and tan brick lanes.

He found the right building, a two-story grey building nestled along the canal. He sat down outside and waited for M to arrive. The small rush of water from the canal was soothing, the far-away noises of the bustling high street and of commuters was reassuring. Of what, the boy didn't know. It was effortless, to sit still and quiet, on the bench outside M's building, quietly waiting. This is what he did all day at school, so the solitude was familiar. Then a dark shape came speeding on bike from around the corner. M was there: dark hair, full beard, short stature; it seemed to be as the picture promised. He stopped by the boy and introduced himself, the softness of his voice incongruent with his aura's wildness. The boy stood up, smiling, and followed M inside. The white hallways were clean, sterile, and exuded a burrowing chill. Cold room here, damp weather there, night falling earlier and earlier; this pattern contributed to the deepening depression that was augmented by too much free time and lonely days. The boy followed M to his flat, where he opened the door and led the boy inside.

The inside was just more livable than outside; the blank walls and disarray of boxes were indicative of a new tenant. M stowed the bike in the spare room and the boy wandered into the living room, where the window overlooked the dreary canal. Small talk was made, and M went to freshen up after his commute home from the banking world of central London. The boy wandered into the bedroom. The mattress lay on the floor, illuminated by the harsh yellow light of a cheap desk lamp with the Primark tag still attached. Framed posters lay against a wall and clothes were piled in a corner. A bachelor pad, as they would say back home. But the boy wasn't home. He was in a stranger's flat thousands of miles from the family that kept track of his communication every day, after the cataclysmic spiel that followed him across the Atlantic a month prior.

The bedroom reminded the boy vaguely of something contrived by a starving artist, or maybe a scientist preparing for a dissection. M came back silently and his hands found the boy's waist and he turned him around. The boy tasted the mint toothpaste on M's breath and the sweat and musk on his skin. The boy's head was led from lips to neck, from neck to chest, chest to nipple, nipple to armpit, and back to lips. Silent submission, under M's direction, under the guiding force of his broad, hairy hand: a contract becoming alive. The boy's eyes didn't focus on anything but remained closed, as the darkness hid the convicting proof of sight. If he couldn't see it, it couldn't be as real. It was only something he was a spectator to, from within a viewing room in his mind, watching his body go through the motions outlined by earlier precedents. M's intensity was interrupted occasionally by a sudden detour by his tongue into the boy's nostril; the sudden interruption was a burst of clarity in an otherwise-familiar cycle of meet, submit, leave, repeat. The sudden penetration of M's cold, wet tongue was a small awakening, but nothing strong enough to penetrate the heavy, cloudy fog around the suffocating conscience in the boy's mind.

M held on to the boy's face with strong grip, his lips moving without compassion. The contract to be fucked hard was beginning to become complete. M forced the boy against the wall, pants coming down around his ankles. M held on to the back of the boy's neck to retain firm grip and control of the thrusts, moans erupting as he pushed as far as the boy's constricting throat would allow. M's rough hands rubbed up and down the boy's slender frame, preparing meat for the cut. The boy knew what came next in the cascade, that the finale was drawing near. But nothing could provoke the rebellion inside to overcome the heaviness of the cycle, nothing could overpower the cloudy, murky film. He was pushed down to the floor at the mattress' edge as M ripped open a condom and proceeded without permission or lubrication. The boy felt the throbbing pain on his insides and the scrapes of dry friction, but no objection or scream or cry or plea escaped his lips. Only silence, pre-programmed by what would continue the cycle and let him to survive. The boy prayed to the god he'd rejected long ago that M would come quickly; that it would end soon. With every thrust was a small parcel of hope, maybe the next time is the last, maybe he'll be done with me soon. *Maybe it'll stop hurting soon, maybe I won't want to die in two minutes.* The boy's chin was arched so that it was crammed against the ridge of the mattress; the light of the lamp was burning into his eyes as M performed to the rhythm of a fast-paced drum. M's hands held on to the boy's body, commanding submission. The boy melted into the comfort of oblivion as the beat grew rougher and faster, a drum beat of invaders of a lost civilization, as the pain didn't go away and as hope died another futile death. M finally finished, fell forward onto the boy's body, and locked the boy into an inescapable embrace.

The embrace was a prison that the boy's heart was screaming for him to leave, to gather his clothes and to run home to bed where he could fall apart, be hurt, to hurt himself, and bleed. But no, he remained silent in

M's strong grasp. The wide space between his
screaming mind and the unresponsive neurons started
to shrink, the battle between conscious drive and the
cycle was finally ending. And then M said it was time
for the boy to go, to get back home forty-five minutes
west across the city. As the boy dressed, trying to hide
how his legs and arms were shaking with cold and
shame and exhaustion, M remarked about how fun
he'd had and how he'd like to hang out again. The boy
responded with sound and a nod in lieu of a coherent
response as he left.

The boy wandered back to the bus stop, legs and
insides sore and feeling out of touch with the physical
world around him. Was any of this real? Was what
happened real? Was he even alive? What was
overwhelmingly real was the settling, enveloping
shame and disappointment that the cycle had
completed, that it had even started at all. The boy's
mind couldn't escape the smell of M's sweat and musk,
the carnal smell of sex, the stickiness on his skin, and
the soreness and growing exhaustion emanating from
his core. The boy boarded the bus in a daze, not really
remembering how to get home. He got off the bus too
early out of fear that the other people on the bus could
smell what he had done. He wandered down the street
in an unfamiliar neighborhood and hoped that he could
get home without falling down and melting into the

concrete. He finally found a glowing, red and blue sign and descended the stairs into Bethnal Green station. The smell of sex was still on his hands and beneath his shirt, but the heaviness of the stifled underground air provided a cover so that the convicting evidence was only noticeable to the boy.

He sank into a seat and let the stops of the Central Line fall away along his regular commute home, only one stop shorter this time. He climbed the escalators to the exit and walked silently up the street to the white row house he called home. That he still thinks of as a home.

The housemates asked where he'd been, how was his day, and he uttered robotic replies, regurgitated pleasantries as his mind had once-again defaulted to auto-pilot. He lay down on the blue carpeted floor in the living room, aching to melt into the floor and to be free of these things that never seemed to stop, no matter how strongly he felt after the completion of each reiteration.

He found solace in the darkness of his room, opening the little window overlooking the garden. The noise of trains passing through the Notting Hill Gate station on the District and Circle lines was comforting, a rhythmic interruption in the silence of the room. His cold bed welcomed him home, the dark space opened up to the memories he wanted to shed. He fell asleep, maybe. He can't remember just what happened; if he cut himself, if he cried, if he purged, if he felt anything at all.

processional (november 2014)

The darkness is omnipresent, the cold air filling in the spaces between the layers of clothing on my body. The chilling wind nips at my eyes, my nostrils, my ears; its frigid bite reminds my body that it is alive. It is present, it is here. My feet fall upon the damp, wet stones that comprise the pathway along the south bank of the Thames. My lungs inhale the cold, biting air and exhale carbon dioxide into the city's spaces. My hands are stuck in the pockets of my olive-green coat with the faux-fur lining. My eyes glisten with something that's deeper than simply love for this city. My eyes glisten with the realization that I am alive and that I am in a city that for me, only existed in an imaginary realm only two months ago. The lights of the city around me illuminate the otherwise dark stage upon which the day is concluding. The early days of winter are fleeting and growing ever shorter; with that, the nights and the absence of celestial illumination grow more familiar.

I pull myself back into a less fanciful reality, one where the coldness of the pavement isn't romantic. The cold seeps up through my boots as I walk down the river bank as the distance between his advancing figure and mine remains constant. He faces straight ahead; his hands are in the pockets of his overcoat and his blonde hair is partially obscured by his toboggan. The darkness that fell so early in the cold city creates a shadow that permeates universally. I can't distinguish the hem on the back of his coat, or where the pockets are on his Levi's. The longer that I stare at the back of his coat as he continues to walk eastwards along the Thames, the idea of him starts to grow muddled around its edges in my mind—much like how words lose their meaning the longer you focus your attention upon them, repeating them endlessly in your head. As minutes pass, my perception of him dulls, but with the waning comes an unexpected numbing of something I can't identify. But I can clearly feel the accompanying sense of disquiet, even though my body still moves robotically, placing my feet in the shadows of his footsteps. It takes a breed of faith, instilled in me by a force other than my own volition, to continue the procession down the concrete streets.

We reach the Tate Modern after walking through the courtyard with the trees lit with small, white holiday lights and through the boardwalk below the OXO building. We walked past Blackfriars and its signs advertising an impending closure for renovations. We walk past the tourists that stop to take the obligatory photos of the illuminated city along the river and we walk past the lovers settled on secluded benches facing the river. We walk past everything with an inexplicable hurry. He turns right and ascends the clear glass of the access point to the Millennium Bridge; he has still yet to look back at me.

This is my walk, the one I complete daily on my way home from school. This is my space, a sanctuary for a new-found religion. In its daily practice, I commence my pilgrimage at Waterloo and wander down Southbank until I reach the Millennium Bridge, where I stride across the Thames in the wake of the illuminated St. Paul's Cathedral. This is my dutiful presentation for a secular type of ethereal judgment: I stand on the bridge, solemnly present and wholly displayed for the city to see. When alone, this is my time to be reduced to something diminutive by the building that sits so prominently, so astutely, so regally, and so resoundingly whole. As I cross the bridge alone, memories are recovered, scars are revealed, and my eyes are fixated on the gleaming white marble of the church. It is my time of atonement, of reconciliation, of hope that there is something as beautiful as this moment to be found and treasured in my future. This is my walk, my place, my time to look inwards at myself and to try my best to accept what I see.

But now, I must hurry across the bridge in the wake of the man I met a few weeks ago. Instead of feeling the harbored grief and confusion and memories fall away into the dark waters below, they swirl around me, pleading for a release that I can't provide. We reach the cobblestone steps on the other side of the bank. He starts up the stairs, walking towards the Tube station that will lead us to our respective homes. I don't think he looked back. I feel the physical effects of my exertion taxing my breaths; they become labored, constrained, and I feel less like me.

In this moment, as my lagging distance increases to six, seven feet, I suddenly feel myself duck down an alley to the right, past the office building made entirely of glass. I don't know why this happens, there's only a nanosecond of premeditation before I find my body following the invisible hook that pulls me off the center stage. I hide in the darkness of the small alley in the shadow of the cathedral, and I feel my lungs expand with piercing cold air. He's no longer in my field of vision. He's no longer leading me along his quiet march. He's no longer staring at me with blatantly condescending blue grey eyes, rolling them backwards in his head as he turns back to the allure of his iPhone screen on the train back from Watford. He's no longer silently fuming about his credit card being declined at the gift shop, storming out in silence and leaving me wondering if this means he'll later take out his anger on me. He's no longer silent when I ask questions or share stories from my life across the pond. He's no longer vigilantly surveying the area around us before he tries to kiss me, his tongue trying to force its way in to the warm refuge of my mouth. His inexperience causing him to hesitate, to falter. His hands reflecting his lack of interest, his lack of drive, as they remain motionless, barely touching my hips. The anxious pressure in my chest solidified during the trip to Watford and now, in this this alley, it diffuses through my skin into the cold air. I am free in this moment, having escaped the invisible ropes that held me tied to him, like a bound hostage being pulled to my next hiding place.

Analogous to an animal that suddenly finds its cage unhinged, the latch somehow broken, its freedom sitting silently on the forest floor mere steps outside of the cage, I begin to evaluate the parameters of my freedom. My body instinctually moves toward another Tube station via back streets and alleys that I know intimately. I know where I can access the Central line that will take me back to the safety of the white row house in Pembridge Gardens, to friends that won't know what happened, to friends that won't know to ask, but to friends that I can smile for, I can laugh with, friends whom I can use as a barrier against what

happened today. But then as I turn a corner, and there
he is. I see that I had made my way back to the
processional path, that my body had betrayed my
momentary liberation. I see him standing maybe 20
feet away and my heart sinks a little deeper than it was
before, as I realize that the corporeal packaging of my
spirit followed the instructions of another. Maybe my
body subconsciously found its way back to him, only
allowing itself a temporary reprieve. He sees me and as
he moves forward, he asks why I'd disappeared, what
the hell I thought I was doing. My mouth dumps a
garbled excuse, something I wouldn't remember
saying two minutes afterwards. We board the Central
line at St. Paul's station, and we sit in utter silence as
the train takes us westward. I get off at Notting Hill
Gate and he continues on to some stop off of the Circle
Line, maybe Goldhawk Road. I don't look back as I
step onto the platform and move with the hordes of
people exiting the station to return to their homes,
their families, their respite. I feel numb, I feel nothing.
I walk and walk and then I'm home.

I never saw him again. I never texted, never called. I
knew as I walked away from him at the tube platform
that I could find that freedom again, that somehow, I
could outsmart the grip that my disease had on my
body. Years later, I can't quite remember the contours
of his face, but I will never forget the spike of

rejuvenating elation that I felt as I ducked down the alleyway. I felt the golden kiss of freedom, of autonomy, of control. I will never forget how pure and how right it felt to have it run through the course of my veins, nor will I forget the disappointment I felt as I saw my body lead me back to him.

I may forget his body, his face, the things that he said to me that made me feel inadequate and silly and stupid and alone, but I will never forget what I felt. Those things are etched in permanent ink on the inside of my skin, along my organs, along my vessels, in the firing of my neural networks, in me.

You can never forget how true freedom feels and how it feels to lose it.

a question i couldn't answer (december 2014)

Tomás asked me why I did it. I don't really remember
what I was feeling or thinking before I left last night; I
just remember suddenly finding myself leaving and
going to this Canadian's flat in Kensington. I
remember how he was gentle and sophisticated; he was
initially hesitant to kiss me but then time accelerated
and I clearly remember being gagged as he pushed
down into my throat. "*Your throat is almost opened up*",
he said, as if pushing past my gag reflex down into my
esophagus with his cock was something of which to be
proud. I remember tears in my eyes that never fell
down my face as I saw myself swallowing him and
hoping that I wouldn't choke or vomit. He was soft
with how he touched me with his hands, but there was
still his hardening desire that I couldn't ignore. I was
being fucked; there was no other way to frame it. He
entered me without a condom and it hurt at first. He
stopped as my face contorted as I couldn't hide that
pain. He then said he "*couldn't fuck me because he would
cum almost immediately*" and I didn't respond. I couldn't
vocalize what was in my mind; I told myself to stop, to
put my clothes on, to go home, to stop putting myself
at risk. He pulled out after a few thrusts that hit that
place inside me that still doesn't feel quite right; the
spot serving as a reminder that someone was fucking

me and that I was being used to fulfill man's calling to dominate and to inseminate. I can't say that I didn't feel physical pleasure because I did. I felt good at times but I knew in the rational part of my mind that it was wrong, that I was betraying myself and I was betraying Tomás and those who I've promised that I would take care of myself. The man told me he knew how I'd react, and he was right—the panic attack hit just as he finished. I don't have any other choice than to trust what he tells me, at this point. At least he treated me like a person. At least my face was only pressed down into the carpet for only a short while before he pressed the twenty-pound note into my hand and told me to go home.

Tomás asked me why I did it, to which I replied: *"I don't think I have an immediate answer to this, but I think I finally gave in to the recurring impulse to go back to how I used to act (or as I still do, as last night proves) in a mindset of immaturity and ignorance of the potential consequences of what I was doing. I was being selfish, in a self-involved, pitying, destructive manner. I wasn't really present mentally; I was shirking personal responsibility and I don't honestly know why I did it, I don't really remember what I was feeling last night."*

And then he replied: *"I'm just so afraid that you hate yourself and I feel like for the first time in my life I'm beginning to love myself and I just want to give that to you. But I don't know how...if I had done what you did last night, it would have been out of insecurity."*

Embarrassed, I said: *"does insecurity mean self-hatred, though?"*

"Ya, I think it does," he said.

I stammered: *"hate is just a really strong word."*

Tomás: *"It was a pretty strong action."*

Is he right, do I hate myself? Do I want myself to suffer, to writhe, to be defeated, to be fucked, reduced, manipulated, and broken? Is that what I want? Is it because I truly hate myself? Do I hate myself?

somewhere in notting hill (17 december 2014)

I left you somewhere in Notting Hill
The interdependence, the intertwine
The taste we didn't like but couldn't redefine
Remember when you arrived, remember how you felt
The first time you walked down our street
Did you feel yourself start to fall apart?

I left you somewhere in Notting Hill
I can't pinpoint the day, but I feel it still
There's a deadness in a silent part of me
I'll guard it forever, suppressing it reverently

I saw you again last night, and it took me by surprise
I didn't like the feeling of it fighting to be alive
It took control and I felt like I did before
I was embarrassed and felt like I owed myself more
I owe myself more

I left you somewhere in Notting Hill
And that's where you need to stay
I left that place without your grip around my throat
Is this what it's like to breathe?

the red carpet : un roman à clef (part two)

The boy went abroad and had a nervous breakdown. But he found help: a therapist who invited him into her cozy home in Primrose Hill, the medicine that changed his life drastically, and the new friendships with housemates. He started to feel alive again, better than he had in a long time. Being in London made him feel okay, even after hiccups and nightmares found where he was hiding.

He got drunk one night and wrote S a letter, telling him that he couldn't feel guilty for S's problems. That he didn't want to room with him again, that he couldn't even be his friend.

As the semester abroad ended, it came time for students returning from abroad to being spring housing registration. The boy was allocated to the last slot, which meant he would have one and only one choice for housing, as there were exactly enough bed spaces for the male students coming back from abroad that semester. He logged on and saw the open space and his heart stopped. The listing was for the Theatre house, a double room, with S. He had never wanted this, to have to live with him again. He shut down, instead of speaking up and finding a way out, he was silent. He swallowed his bitter disbelief and tried to suppress his burgeoning fear while his mother and cousin visited him during his last week in England.

He didn't receive a reply to the message he sent S.

The boy's new boyfriend, Tomás, helped move him into the Theatre house. He was very afraid. But S wasn't there at first, so he quickly moved in his things and left. He and Tomás stopped by later so that he could grab a charger and S was there, in bed, in the same brooding position as the boy remembered. He didn't say a word to the boy or Tomás. Minutes after they left, the boy received a text saying they needed to talk before he continued moving in. The boy was scared.

They did talk. S said this was not going to work. The boy said he had no other option. S accused the boy of doing this on purpose, to which the boy had no new response. He never wanted this. The boy said they would have to make it work, he guessed. S said he'd been trying to get him moved ever since the first message, but the school wouldn't help. S said that the boy being there would make him angry and angrier, as would Tomás coming and going. S said he didn't know what would happen to all that anger, what it would make him do. With this said, he turned to look the boy directly in the eyes, the gaze from his dark, beady eyes piercing through the space between them.

The boy was terrified, the threat being obvious and blatant. He fled; he cried in his car, forced to tell his parents what was going on (to an extremely limited extent: *my roommate threatened me because he had feelings for me and I didn't reciprocate*). He called upon administrators, looking for help. A bed had opened up incidentally that afternoon in a fraternity suite on campus—there was now a place for him to go. He was able to move out the next day.

That night, he lay awake. S had gone somewhere, and the boy was afraid to fall asleep. What would happen if he wasn't on his guard? Around 3:00 AM, S entered and stood in the doorway for several minutes, for too long, gazing the boy's supposedly sleeping body. Then he closed the door and darkness overwhelmed the room. The boy's heartbeat was furious and rapid, threatening to breach the constraints of his ribs. Falling asleep meant that he could be taken by surprise, that he could be hurt again. He was afraid, more afraid than he'd ever been in his life.

The boy's friends slowly found out what had happened and protected him on campus, warning him when to keep his head down or to turn the other way. The semester wasn't easy, but he survived. He did well in classes, survived the endless cycles that plagued him multiple times a week, and tried to find new ways to feel alive.

S messaged him at the end of the year asking for reparations, to make things better, to make peace. The boy was hurt, shocked, silent. He never responded.

It happened again at the beginning of the fall: another Facebook message that was sent through blocked profiles and phone numbers. The same message, saying that S wasn't angry anymore and couldn't live with himself unless he made peace. Still the boy was silent.

When he saw S in pictures on Facebook, or walking on campus, the boy was still afraid, very afraid. But he told himself being this close to S on a daily basis was temporary.

All things are transitory, he told himself. *You survived that, you survived the cycles, you are working to heal from all these things. These men, S included, will not win. I am a survivor, I will survive.*

A week after I first wrote a draft of this account, I woke up screaming from a nightmare in which S was able to finish what he started on that night in May, angrily and forcefully, with furious vengeance in his eyes. But this won't happen. Nightmares don't have to become truth. Dreams don't have to be real.

3 january 2015

Tomás: Do you know how to relax?
Me: No.

part two

the hurting

"…he has the sensation he always had…that his body
was not his own, that every gesture he made was
predetermined, reflex after reflex after reflex, and that
he could do nothing but succumb to whatever might
happen to him next."
-Hanya Yanagihara, *A Little Life*

argentine

You tell me you feel the sadness, arising at the same
time every night

A creature familiar to both of us, to which we can give
a worn-out name

Contrary to what you try to sell to the watching world

I think you're human, open to the mistakes we've both
made
In-between three worlds, the old the new and the now
You tell me you left your heart in Buenos Aires, but
this story existed there too
So now in this small town we're forced to confront
these sad territories, things that clog the exiting of
lymph from our souls

The atoms that separate us tell us the things we don't
wish to remember

When we close our eyes, we see the films we made but
can't bear to burn

I hold you close, praying to a godless expanse that I
can help you wipe the slate clean

And one night, we collide and these things intertwine
and ravage and fall away
replay: sad days, sad eyes and I think our hearts are
sad too

But I think we can find a place where those words
don't tumble out in confessions meant to prove
inadequacy and a winner in sorrow

It's not Argentina; you are here, but I'm here, too.

5 february 2015

Overhead from a hallmate

Guy 1: How does she give consent?
Guy 2: I don't know, who needs it anyway. We both
know she wants it.
Me:

21 february 2015

I feel toxic, as if there's poison in my bloodstream that seethes deep into my bones when I'm caught off guard & my defense system can't keep the toxicity at bay. There's an entrenched feeling of being unsettled and of being taken advantage of by the people in my life and of having something stalking me, and if I turn around too quickly I might see it. This fuels the toxic bursts, I think. I don't think it's loneliness, because I honestly don't mind being alone. I need it sometimes.

written at the end of saturday (march 2015)

There's something underlying the hangover, critical
and serious

There's something malignant about how I feel and
how I remember

All of the times I've slipped into

A surreal state, a witnessed reality from which I can't
escape

I'm risking my life and erecting a divide

Between what was done and who I want to be

It's distressing, reducing, silencing

When you can't trust yourself

Enveloped in the conflicts of the person who inhibits
my body

For the fatiguing immensity of the accompanying
emotions

I proclaimed that I am free, I've written it in my skin

But who am I free from?

Free from the nights I've moved in a catalytic trance?

I still feel intoxicated, my head is swimming

In the things that I don't tell, the things that remain

I don't know how to communicate what I don't feel

I rip away at my body because I don't feel anything

The torn flesh, poor retribution for not loving myself?

I don't remember why this ever started

I don't know why it still remains

Cyclic, repeating, replaying, entrancing my rationality

I've divorced and rejoined and melted and bled

Here I go again, with everything to lose.

flashback: the little house in the mist

My memory entombed you with positive physical
feelings; I liked how you liked me. But every time I
was with you in your room, where the stink of dog
permeated infinitely, where the cold breeze from the
fan blew directly at my face in your bed, I remembered
that these memories are falsified, propaganda from a
hijacked region of my mind. Memories can lie, and for
me, they have often. The day that you went too far,
that wasn't the first time it had happened, I remember
now.

6 april 2015

I feel like I'm losing grip; it's like I'm not even real, not
substantial. I'm just a spectator behind my eyelids and
nothing I want or say matters to what I see happen.
The bad thoughts circle in and out, taunting me with
the comfort of entertaining them. Or at least cutting
open the skin on my arms to feel the screams of my
mangled flesh, that's when I feel something that
validates that I am real.

18 June 2015

Today I had my first session with Bernie. Maybe this is all real, after all. Maybe it's not my fault. The tests I took confirmed his diagnosis: PTSD, trauma-associated sex addiction. I'm afraid of what those words mean about me. But I can't dwell on this, I have to take the MCAT in three days. Then I can think about it.

bound (*at last, turning away from the white house*)

It happened and all I can do is take things day by day.
Once you're in New York I won't see you again. That's
comforting, I think.

But then again, I've said it before. This is why I'm
afraid of myself, why I don't trust myself.
You snapchat me occasionally, pictures from life at
Columbia.
Pictures that I never asked for, pictures that I've never
wanted.

Any good memory from before cannot supplant what
you did. The last day we were together finally
dissolved the idolized image I held in my mind. What
you did to me, with the ropes and leather and chains, I
will never forget how it felt.

What kind of life is this, sinking into a feeling of being
safe, and then having that ripped open with an
uninvited intrusion into my life? Not only with you,
but with everyone I never want to see again.

I deserve to feel okay, to feel better, to not feel used, or
simply tolerated, or treated as a disposable play-thing.

But every time I go to therapy with Bernie, the smell of the old Victorian home that houses his office smells just like you. The smell of old wood and history; it's as intoxicating as ever.

a recipe

Step 1: Stand up, because you're unable to sit still in your seat. Your restless heart and your mind that's catapulting through a cascade of worry won't let you stay still for much longer.

Step 2: Pace. Try to release the mounting power through mechanical movements, repeated, in circles, feeling how heavily you step upon the ground in order to jar it out of your system.

Step 3: Realize that it's not working. Feel the new wave of panic hit you. It hits hard.

Step 4: Go to the kitchen, like you knew you would when this all started. You feel something greater than yourself pulling you along a perfectly linear trajectory, there's nothing you have to do but to follow your body to the end.

Step 5: Open the container, pour it all out, shovel it in your mouth as fast as you can. It's like you're committing a crime and if you're caught, it'll all unravel or combust and that's not a risk you can take.

Step 6: When you pause, you immediately revert to the pull to keep eating. Eat. Eat. Eat. Eat. And some more.

Your stomach tightens, it feels like a brick, but you can't stop now. You're almost there.

Step 7: You finish, and finally you can rest. A transitory rest. The small moment between an inhale and an exhale. The quiet moment in which you think that maybe this will end now, five steps early.

Step 8. The pull is back, and you find yourself walking to the bathroom.

Step 9: You prepare for the big event, *le denouement*, the spectacle that you've been working towards. You sink to your knees, bowing before the porcelain shrine. The lid lifts, and you look at the clear water waiting for your sacrifice.

Step 10. This takes some effort. Simply putting fingers down your throat doesn't work any longer; your body has had time to sensitize to this stimulus. You have to apply vigor and force and add a newfound depth to your probing in order to generate the response you seek.

Step 11: You let your body purge itself, of everything you forced into it, and hopefully of the things you can't reconcile or release on your own. You pray to every deity, the ones your parents raised you to worship and the ones you haven't tried yet, you pray that maybe this time you'll finally feel relief.

Step 12: You stand, flush the toilet, you wash out your mouth, dry the tears from your eyes, blotting them to help the redness vanish. When you're done, you walk back to the desk where you're supposed to be answering the phone, this is your job, after all.

11 july 2015

No recovery is perfect, is it? My heart aches.

18 july 2015

Me: 1, The Reaper, 0

I made it through last night without succumbing to an influence greater than my desire to be okay again.

flashback: another summer night, another bmw

I fought against it as long as I could. I tried to keep
you from getting in and it almost worked. I almost felt
victorious. But then you grabbed me and flipped me on
my stomach and fucked me, my face shoved into the
pillows on your bed. I stared into the black expanse,
my mind was far away and was watching as my body
was used as a tool to reach a climax, and hoped that I
would get out alive.

unanswered prayer (july 2015)

There were a thousand things running through my
mind
My face buried into your bedspread
My vision consumed by a black canvas
I didn't want to watch you as you did these things
Your harsh face, a fearful reminder of what I'd had

I tried holding my breath to see if that would make it
better
But then I couldn't ignore the event any longer
The scraping feeling of the pain I've tried to process
But I can't, so I try to recreate it again for another
chance

I prayed to the god I don't believe in
Asking for help to find a way out
But no, I was still there and he said
"I want to fuck you, fuck you hard"

I used all my strength to keep you out
But I could only hold back for so long
I was hoping you'd give up eventually
That my inability to fight back would be relieved

I left smelling like your lube

And blood collecting from where you were
At least you used a condom, that's the silver lining
That sometimes soothes internal writhing

A comedian once made a joke about something similar,
They called it "a little bit of r---"
But they don't get it
A little bit can really fuck over your head.

Now you're another name on the list
An addition to the revelatory number
It makes me want to hate myself-- because blame falls
on no other

The pain doesn't only strike at my core
Because I've been in this place before
The faces circle in a thorny halo--faces that I can't ever
let go

A sad song, and one people get tired of hearing
But the moments that flash forward, never
disappearing
You've got to find a way to live with the monster
That lives down under the thinnest layer of scarring
You've got to live with it, but don't let it out

22 august 2015

It hurt but it always hurts, I'm used to that. I made it end as fast as it could. Get it over with as fast as possible, that was my strategy for surviving an episode. On my way out you asked to see me again and I said yeah, and I fell out the door (literally, because I tripped over the doorstep and looked even more like a fool) and tried not to think the judgmental, hateful thoughts that come at the end of an episode as I drove home. But they always come, just like I can't tell an episode is coming until I'm already under its trance. Today I told Sophie about my diagnosis and she told me it will be okay. She said that addiction and PTSD are strong words, that this is hard to digest. She said I would overcome this. But I don't know how, when I can't tell when it's coming.

1 september 2015

I won't hate myself for what happened. I am still a good person. I will be okay.

eigengrau

I wonder how to make an incapacitated numbness end

I hide the scars of midnight consumption
Evidence of an intimate malfunction

I dare you to have found another way to unwind
The miles of thoughts, burgeoning secrets crammed
into my mind

The discontent, the dissociation
The retribution and the denunciation

Of something more dangerous than what I hide
The lies superimposed upon the scars I tried to force
inside

But scars nestle themselves in the crook of my arm
Juxtaposed by an empowering promise in ink, damning
evidence of self-inflicted harm

I felt calm, watching small rivers dance and flow, but
something felt inherently wrong
But I did what I had to do to and probability allowed
me to move along

A cyclic crippling, depicting a line curving back upon
itself
I called for a companion, but didn't quite understand
how they could help

I believe that this darkness is tangible, something to be
touched
But to be understood by others not quite as much

The comfort the grey space allows
A vision created by my own perception, the deepest
gray of eigengrau

Darkness has a color, darkness has a name
But how to tell the story when no darkness is truly the
same

Do I want to attach words to something so innately
inherent?
Can I make the reality of what's happened justly
apparent?

When is it too soon to reduce memories to words?
To something people can digest, can understand,
something that can be palatably heard.

It's something I can't even really feel, but something I
know

Forgiveness for myself that I've struggled to
genuinely show

But the comfort the grey space allows,
It's somewhere I never have to explain why or how
A vision created by my own perception, the deepest
grays of eigengrau
A trust I'll never doubt

flashback: his husband wasn't home

I felt myself staring blankly into the dark expanse,
thinking *I just want to die*, as I once again couldn't
escape this recurring nightmare that always seemed to
overpower my will and drive to recover. I felt the pain
and the full dullness inside me and I felt something
slowly ripping. Then your thrusts grew faster and you
came in me without a condom, without asking first.
You showed me the door, and my blood followed me
home.

the day i will never forget (19 september 2015)

This is the day I met you.

flashback: when we're together it feels so good to be touched by someone I love and trust. and then I see one of those faces I can't rid myself of and my body contracts and screams and I feel it all over again. You hold me as I sob and shake, you hold me every time and you don't let go.

quatre secrets à l'encre.

un: *mon corps ne me trahira jamais*

I chose this during a time when I believed that
everything was my fault, that the problem stemmed
from an inability to reconcile my mind and body. What
better way to guilt yourself into change than through
permanence? *See right hipbone.*

deux: *je suis libre*

A promise, an aspiration, a dream that one day could
come true. A trophy of the day that I came out to my
mother on the balcony of our hotel room. Sometimes I
wish that I always felt free, that this tattoo, written in
my own handwriting, reflected an unwavering truth.
See inside of left forearm.

trois: *le cercle*

A tribute to the cycles that have defined the last four
years and a representation of the hijacking of my spirit,
my body, and my life. *See right ribcage.*

quatre: *le arbre*

It was never a simple task to love the skeletal framework, the basal truth, the barren tree. But acceptance can be developed and nurtured into something analogous to love. *See left bicep.*

6 october 2015

"You seem to be underreporting. I kept wanting to tell you it's not your fault."

-Bernie, after reading the first draft of my Chronicle

25 october 2015

Last night I went for a late-night drive when I couldn't
fall asleep and needed to get out. I thought about all
the places I can't bear to see any longer in this city.
There are too many places I don't want to go back to.
Too many places where parts of me are missing,
hiding, inaccessible, degraded.

the overlap

"Do you want to leave? Want to go somewhere else?"

Bar trivia had ended; the back room of the pub was packed, the din of competing conversations was growing increasingly louder and the booth that held too many people was growing uncomfortably hot. The beer glasses were empty and our bill was paid. Outside promised the night, fresh air, escape into something less constricting and somewhere a deep breath might be found.

I said yes, yes I would.

We waited for Margo and her friends to figure out where they'd be going, but they were indecisive. Which bar will have the most single guys? Which bar will be the most fun? Where are the others going? They defaulted by ordering another round of beer. I don't drink beer, so we left.

We walked out of the first bar, the girls at the other booths staring at the beautiful man by my side. Six-foot five of slender, muscular flesh. Sharp cheekbones, a stride as powerful as any runway model. Eyes softer than the grey mist of the wintered sea. Long bony hands framed by gold rings and a tortoiseshell-patterned watch. Hair pulled back into a bun, the sleek undercut visible. His reddening skin indicative of his desire to leave, to escape the claustrophobic gathering.

We walked down the street to the next bar. Almost holding hands. But in this town, holding hands is a revolutionary emblem. A reason for a rebuttal, an accusation, an attack. I am a rebel, but the one that hides in the underbrush and skirts the open battlefield. I am a quiet rebel, one that can see the limits and does not challenge the limit alone. Let someone else take the fall first, then challenge the limits when the resounding wave of support emerges. Let the wave carry you forward.

We get to the second bar and go downstairs, where the cool darkness was comforting, cloaking. I felt the boundaries between myself and the air around me blur slightly, and I'm not longer distinct. I can breathe. My body no longer feels out of place, as if I misread the invitation and the directions and ended up at a party of people who hadn't invited me but don't say anything to make me leave. We sit at the bar, in swiveling chairs close enough for our legs to touch. I exhale, inhale, and I look him in the eyes and see the glimmer that's paralyzing, entrancing, intoxicating. He smiles at me, his crooked, bleached smile evoking a warmth from down in my chest, one that I can't command myself.

We order our first round. Paul buys something bitter, he generally avoids sugar, the sweetness is overwhelming to his stomach, he said. I order a Long Island, looking to lose the headache stretched between my temples. A rubber band that's been held back all day, gaining soreness but never losing the potential to snap and burn the fingers that grow tired of holding it steady.

The chatter around us begins to build, the room fills with beautiful people and their beautiful friends. People from school, people from town, they all converge in the bar and it becomes full and loud but the darkness preserves my comfort. I watch the bartender conduct her magic, creating drinks with delicate citrus garnishes and swirling mixtures with liquors from the top shelf. She breaks a bottle, accidentally, and laughs. The sound of breaking glass is a staccato awakening from a reverie I'd not realized I'd sunk into. I see Paul is talking to someone I think he goes to school with; I sit in silence, sipping my drink diligently, listening to the room that's come alive around me. Letting that life fill me. Margo finally catches up to us and throws her arms around my chair and I'm smiling, a bit tipsy.

The glittering skulls on the shelf above the back-corner twinkle in the semi-darkness as I try to keep up conversation with Margo and the others that stand around me, my mouth smiling and forming words and contortions that are unplanned, but fall according to some hidden innate algorithm. I can't feel conscious steerage of what my mouth is saying, my mind is watching what is happening and it happens, over and over again. I lose recollection of what I've just said immediately and I am hesitantly sipping my drink, Paul jokingly said I'm not keeping up so I take a gulp, the liquor burning my throat as it falls down my throat. The burn is satisfying.

The night isn't bad. The conversations are still effortless and mechanical, filling the spaces that were earlier seething with hurt. Paul looks over at me, and I feel things align and solidify inside my head. I feel the pull from the middle of my thoracic cavity, yanking me into his dark eyes. The girls walk away, and I turn back into my reverie that I'm sharing with the glittering skulls across from me, their glamour tantalizing me.

Paul interrupts his conversation and leans over to me, his lips brushing my ear.

"Do you see that guy sitting down the bar? I used to sleep with him. He was deep in the closet. We met off Grindr, and he didn't even tell me his name. I looked in his wallet for his ID when he was in the bathroom. He tried to tell me he was bi, that he wasn't really gay, but I told him that was bullshit. He liked me fucking him too much. I wanted you to know in case he came over here to talk to me."

I find a moment to look down the bar at the handsome brunette man sitting a few seats down from me. He's wearing a red and blue checked flannel shirt, his toned body filling it nicely and his presence being of a man who's wary of the room, watching for things that could usurp his station. A middle-food-chain predator, looking down at the prey he could dominate but also listening for the larger, more powerful beasts that could overthrow his diminutive kingdom. I know that look on his face, that aura he exudes. The way his face contorts in response to what his buddies have just said, my own knows that pattern intimately. My face has made those shapes before.

"You like brunettes, don't you?"

"Well duh. Look at you, how couldn't I?"

I take more sips, and then more and more. I realize my drink is almost empty, I can't even taste the liquor anymore. I just taste the sweet lemonade and the fullness of whatever gin was left. I order another Long Island. I drink this one more quickly, trying to hide my glances down the bar to see if I can catch a full glance of this man's face. The profile was all I could glimpse.

That night, we're in bed and my body employs its familiar, contorting response. As he touches me, I see him touching the guy from the bar. I see in my imagination that guy doing the same things and when Paul comes on me, and I see the infinitesimally small molecules that were once in that guy from the bar. I see the millions of molecules that now are all over me, that landed in my mouth and I taste the acid in their punch. I see the ghost of a nonexistent virus, sliding down my sides onto the teal towel he laid on the bed, leaving streaks of sticky wetness of my skin. I see the molecules and their promise on my body. I see them and I know them. I draw them in invisible ink on the back of my eyelids, on the insides of my arms, on the back of my teeth, in the journal that holds all my truths.

I now know a face whose body they also entered, I saw his body and his face and his beard and his hands and his hair and the way he was smiling at the joke his buddy made about a girl he tried to fuck. I see the invisible, hopefully imaginary virus molecules that broke through the endless precautions and medications from another of Paul's ex-lovers, whose viral load was nonexistent but the diagnosis was unwaveringly present. I see all these things in flashes, one after the other, and I lose my breath, I lose it again and again. The pressure in my chest is growing, my lungs are screaming to release the CO_2 dissolved in my bloodstream, to find relief in the intake of a rush of air. I gasp, and I gasp again.

Paul looks at me in the way that leaves me holding my breath, when his eyes twinkle in the way that only I can see, and we kiss. I try not to hold my breath.

"I'm falling in love with you, you know that?" He says this as I stare, unblinkingly, into the dark depths of his eyes where there's something that I'll never be able to touch or hold or identify or give a name. It's there and it holds me tightly, he holds me tighter, and I feel safe in his warmth, those visions fall away to the back corner of my mind where they'll reside until the next time they reappear to perform their rituals in hopes of a greater sacrifice.

"I think I'm falling in love with you, too."

je suis libre (12 november 2015)

I survived.
It's not your fault, it's not your fault, it's not your fault
That's what they tried make me swallow
But after it happened, who else did I have to blame but
myself?

The adults that heard me cry but didn't listen
The counselor who told me that I must have been
mistaken
That what I said aloud didn't make sense
That I shouldn't know the problem without seeing its
solution

Well, take another look at those nights
The ones I unknowingly tried to recreate
In sudden flashes and disjointed memories and
muddled words
But nothing quite accurately depicts it
The flashbacks where I repeatedly relived it

Those reruns, an unwilling return to desecrated spaces
Where no matter how much I wanted to, I couldn't
speak
Where my body betrayed me, over and over again
Where these things were captive within me

Where I made blood run in rivers across my skin
Where I couldn't control the demented creation
Where their faces blazed in my mind
Where I didn't feel real, an inaccessible justice

A spectator up above, the viewer predicts how it will
conclude
And the action follows the anticipated course
My mind was up above, watching the forest burn down
Forced into silence, every fiber of my locked-away
mind ached
For someone, something, anything to end it
To finally feel it all rip apart
To feel that I could be fully validated
In the real world, the one I wake up in

But I survived, I survived, I survive
It's not my fault, it's not my fault, it's not my fault
This is what I'm taught to say
Instructed to let it become engrained
It didn't go down as smoothly as gin, the four-letter
diagnosis
But now it permeates and flows and I can start to
breathe again

The relief from knowing that what corroded my mind
is real
And my memories and my scars aren't fallacies after all

Remember the darkness when the stars stumbled and
fell
In that darkness I prayed to a godless expanse that I
would live
To survive what was happening, and what would
happen again

When my mouth finally found the mechanism to speak
No sentences or words or admissions felt right
Rehearsals and repetitions and trials and silences
Frustration built while friends struggled to
understand
But I finally found words that could liberate captive
forces
The forces and feelings inside that I'll never justly
recreate
But these words fall so hard off the tongue, who wants
to hear them again?

Now in black ink, the cycles that plagued my mind are
on my skin
The ink permanently reduced monsters to words and
symbols
I've taken them back for me, for me, for me
To claim victory over the men who almost won
But unlike a buried ruin, a burned forest can regrow
And it reaches upward from its own ashes

Their faces still stay with me, I live with them every
day
I still see their eyes in flashes on the back of my eyelids

But I survived, I survived, I survive.

8 december 2015

Written on the cover of my journal:

"the sky rained
gasoline instead of water
I ignored the urge
to set myself on fire
and I smiled,
and I felt joy."   -Oliver Nolan

a physician listened

Date: 11 January, 2016

Location: WFU Student Health

Provider: LP, M.D.

Problem List: Tightness in chest and throat, ongoing chest pain, loss of appetite, episodes of binge eating and purging, racing heartbeat, severe temporal headaches, insomnia, practices of self-harm (no suicidal thoughts), restlessness, inability to focus, weekly panic attacks

Plan: EKG, referral to psychiatrist, take referral to emergency scholarship fund for financially-constrained students, referral to additional therapy resources at University Counseling Center, add 2 anxiolytic medications, schedule the final round of HIV/STD testing, prescribe sleeping pills, see once a month through the end of the year.

the logic of a heart (january 2016)

Do you remember the stream
The one that flows gently, water jumping from rock to rock in soft trickles
Telling secrets that fall in the wind
Around the rocks and limb-ridden banks

Do you remember when the snow fell down upon our city, and we went back to that stream
And it was quiet, it was still, it was pure
And I stood and breathed it in, the air, the clarity, I felt myself breathe in everything
I breathed deeply, over and over and in that moment
I realized that I could breathe deeply again

Do you remember the first time
When you ran up the trail ahead of me
The frog that waited patiently as you introduced it to me
I stood behind you as you walked further into the woods
And I knew
Something was different, an unprecedented shift
I felt my lungs expand how they hadn't before
The blood flowing through my circulation felt shaken, its composition slightly rearranged

And a smile erupted, a morning glory at dawn
And what it was, I couldn't say, but I knew

My world had been so carefully arranged
Built on fragile constructs with the goal of restoring
something I believed I'd lost
A ancient forest pillaged and burned
But then I knew, I knew and I felt fear
There's something special that was born
And it flows and breathes and laughs
And it's scary sometimes but it's real
I knew and I know and still
The things that words can't encapsulate
They stay with me, they're with me now
But when I look at you before you wake up,
I know and I feel and I smile.

18 february 2016

My mom came to visit for my birthday, to get lunch
and to spend the day together. I'd had a hard week in
therapy, in anxiety, in everything. After lunch we went
on a walk through Reynolda Gardens and she asked
why I needed to keep seeing Bernie, why him and why
so frequently? I tried to skirt around the truth but it
was too big; I realized that compromising the shroud
of privacy around my life was unavoidable. I told her of
my illnesses, of three of the events that happened. I
didn't want to break her heart again, but I think I did.
We cried together; she was upset that I'd not told her
sooner. She didn't understand the mechanics of it, she
once told me that there wasn't such a thing as "safe
gay sex". I tried to patch things up, to compose myself,
and then I went to class, where I listened to people
argue about the fundamental responsibility of a patient
to advocate for outcomes of their healthcare and all I
could think was *but what if they can't speak at all?*

part three

the healing

"Forgive the trees
For the way they can't stop shaking
Even after all these years of practice.
Forgive yourself
For the days you don't even want to try."
-Y.Z., *A Dying Art*

after the war

Call up your ex-lovers and your fading friends
But most importantly, the ghosts of who you used to
be

Give them your number, tell them to call anytime
To share what they know, they'll figure out what to
say
To add little threads to the ever-growing tapestry
To fill in the blanks that scatter the filling page
To add to the story, the story you still don't believe in
To help you remember, to help you to accept

Because how do you fill in the gaps
When you can't see the depth of the holes
Or where the blank waiting to be filled begins or ends
Or the faces of those people who bore witness to the
war

Holes patched by words not strong enough to keep out
the wind
Chilly bursts swirl and scream and dwell
In how many ways can you recreate your own hell?

None of this was your fault, they say
But the craters tell another story

Of bombs and fires and burnings and little deaths
Leaving behind scars in your heart, your arms
Preserved in films that play at night when you close
your eyes

Those things can't just be filled in and forgotten
These things stay with you every moment of every day

So maybe instead of filling the blanks, of patching the
holes
I'll learn to live with the contours of my new
topography
I'll plot the new mountains and valleys as they rise and
fall
And who the hell says I can't have it all?

16 march 2016

excerpts from a letter I wrote to Grace (in an attempt to mend a friendship I tore apart).

"At what point do you run out of energy to expend? At what point do you fall in on yourself and break? At what point do you give up?..."

"...I went abroad to run away and found that I couldn't run away because the Trauma had hijacked my body and was not limited to my American environment like I'd hoped. My body convulsed and threatened to implode and I clung to whatever I could as to not drown. Witnessing the destruction of a fantasy upon which I'd pinned my survival almost killed me. I had no hope of ever finding myself again, of ever feeling different, of ever healing, of becoming something different, of feeling safe. But I couldn't say any of this. I physically could not speak about it. I was able to speak briefly about small details to a therapist in London that got me into a house in Notting Hill where at least I had people around me to check-in and to make me feel a part of a family. My parents were incredibly upset because all I could tell them was "I don't want to be here, I want to come home". That's all I could really tell anyone, to be honest. That made me feel even more alone than before, but I found a biting solace in the solitude. If I had to suffer, at least no one close to me would be hurt and I was living in a beautiful, wonderful city. A romanticized end, the most beautiful and glorified of sufferings; that's the greatest privilege to obtain, isn't it? But against my best efforts, I continued to suffer from episodes and flashbacks while in England and was assaulted while I was in London. I couldn't tell anyone because I was physically unable to talk about what was happening inside and around me. I still can't tell my therapist the details, I have to write them down and hand them in like a course paper: an 80-page Chronicle. I've written about everything that's happened in an attempt to preserve it somewhere separate from my mind as a last-ditch effort of respite..."

"...I pushed you away for the minute and falsely contrived reason that I pushed a lot of people away. That was what I had control over: who I could push away, what I could destroy of my own volition to counter what was desecrated against my will..."

"...Having a name assigned to my illness, my experience, my fear: that in itself increased the severity and weight. But it wasn't until I had these names and diagnoses that I was able to start the process of recovery. It wasn't until I could learn that what was happening to me was very much real and not at all anything I could control that I was able to see that I will live with some fragment of the Trauma for the remainder of my life. Will it always be difficult and painful? Not always, I hope. The process of healing involves ripping open the flesh and festering wounds in order to give them space to fully breathe, to scream and writhe in pain. Then the scar tissue can form, and another region is ripped open. This process is repeated over and over again until I feel my body in all its wholeness again. The pain is not eternal, but the scar tissue will forever be part of my body."

red ribbons (23 march 2016)

The world inverts upon itself
When you turn around
And you look down, you see what wasn't there before
Twisting, suspended, a cobweb of red ribbons
Your heart stops, rises, and constricts and struggles in
your throat
Your stomach drops and forms a knot so it won't tear
itself in two
The last time you faced this apparition
You barely made it out alive
Your body thinks you're back in that place
But you're not
You're safe now
You just have to walk out the door
And go back to his arms
And let him remind you that you're not
there

14 april 2016

The sunshine hit my back with a gentle warmth, a reminder that winter was over. The coldness that had seeped into my bones could begin to break apart, dissipate, fall into a warm puddle at my feet. The wind carried echoes of avian conversations, while spring songs filled my ear canals with joyous, sprightly notes. I watched my feet as I walked along the path, my head down, and I feel myself take a deep breath. It's unhindered, it's almost effortless, it feels unconstrained. I stop my procession and follow with a gasp; this freedom is unprecedented, foreign, even fantastical, almost. I take another deep breath and I can't find the familiar binding of tension and pressure that had wrapped itself as a corset around my chest. I turn around, trying to see if maybe I'd dropped it along my morning walk to class, but all I can see is the brilliant green of fertilized lawn and the yellow residue of pollen on the sidewalk. There's no black clump, no bleeding tumor, no crawling monster. It's just me. I breathe in again, and I realize that I'd forgotten to take my medicine that morning. My mind then arrives at the final destination: I didn't need it this morning. I look up to the sky, almost delusional, and I see a circular shape in the sky slowly move from behind the sun to its own spot in the Carolina blue sky. It's lavender tinted, crater-filled, and I know it's a new moon. Well, not a new moon, it was always there, its orbit perfectly obscured by the glaring brightness of the sun. But somehow its orbit fell apart from the sun, and it's in the sky, alone and present. I close my eyes and I feel the warmth of the sun on my skin along with a cooling trickle that starts in my temples, the site of my usual headaches that fight to split my head open every day, and then the coolness cascades through my thoracic cavity and pools in my feet. The coolness releases my limbs and muscles from tense paralysis, my body falling into a gentle relaxation. I'd not known my body was in frozen contraction until I felt it breathe.

quelque chose que nous ne pouvons pas perdre: une lettre

"When I first really met you (swimming boot camp spring semester 2015!) I was immediately struck by two things: first, your maturity. You called me by my first name right away. Second and most of all, your strong sense of self. At the very least, you seem always to be able to assign words to your emotions. That's not always easy to do, even less so for students. Maybe that's a by-product of counseling. Maybe that's just how you are. Both of these qualities set you far apart from many people your age. Your illness (I have a hard time using that word; maybe because I don't know the extent of it) has given you an emotional vulnerability. But this is where it gets hard for me: if there was one trigger event that set things off for you (and I'm guessing there was), then I don't know if aspects of your personality are a result of it. I doubt it. People don't tend to change in their nature. I recall a moment last year, swimming, when I felt like I had broken through a layer of you and you let out a laugh of pure joy: I had asked you if my 25-free time was faster than Adam's (and since I am documenting things here, I will remind you that it is WAY faster). But just that one laugh, just that once. It was like a rip in the sky and I got to peek through to the other side. Why don't

I see more of that? Maybe I'm simply in the wrong context to see it. Your biggest obstacle? It's not really an obstacle, but you are extraordinarily sensitive to the world around you. That's a good characteristic to have, but not a fun one. It makes you receptive and (when you want to be) open to others, but also makes things harder to shake off. So perhaps there is an aura of melancholy about you at times. But I don't think it defines you, and I also think it speaks to me. It's something that makes you approachable and infinitely lovable. Not in the kitty-cat sense of the word, but rather in the "worthy of love" sense of it. I hope you know that. Appreciate your suffering, both the residue from anything bad that has happened as well as any anticipatory grief you might have about anything bad that is to come. Healing isn't supposed to make you get over your past as much as learn how to incorporate it into your person without letting it chip away at you any further. I was recently discussing with a colleague the state of human rights in North Carolina. In a spinoff from that conversation, I mentioned that over the centuries, social changes in general have resulted in people living happier and more fulfilled lives. We still have a long way to go, globally, but compared to 200 years ago, at least some people can marry outside of their social class, not worry about the baron taking away their hunting rights, get a job regardless of gender, etc. This gets all wildly hypothetical, but I wondered out loud that if humanity ever survives long enough to get to the point at which we all live without pain, without fear, without oppression, will we have still have literature? Think of the great masterpieces. They are all borne of suffering. Who wants to read a novel in which everything is just ducky the whole way through? Apply that idea to people. But not simply in the cliched "we are all authors of our own stories" sense. I suppose we get to create of a lot of the plot, but sometimes we only get to edit, and maybe do some cutting and pasting and thesaurus work. A lot of material gets hurled at us, like it or not. Maybe that means that life is as much about processing as it is about creating. So my advice is to apply this concept of constructive suffering to yourself. The human condition is inherently about suffering. Your past - all of it, your trauma included - has turned you into someone phenomenal. It will be hard to see you leave. Of all the students I have gotten to know, you are the one I will remember with the most joy and the most regret. The former because of who you are; the latter simply because I didn't meet you sooner.

With love,

-    Alyssa

25 april 2015

I started the preparation work for EMDR today. I
identified a true safe place, rather than the safe place of
my past: the darkness and staring past the physical
objects I could see in order to dissociate. Bernie led me
through a bilateral stimulation meditation, the first
step of EMDR. I'm optimistic about the future
processing sessions. I'm ready to feel whole again.
Bernie described the process quite poetically. My mind
is a glass of ice water, and most of my thoughts and
memories are the liquid water, fluid and able to move
and change. There are the ice cubes, though, rigid and
they produce specific responses and can't flow with the
rest of the water. EMDR will help to melt those ice
cubes, to integrate their contents into the rest of the
glass to help things flow smoother.

les visages au-delà du voile

the chorus steps onto center stage

the chorus deliberates:

I do not know what a "solution" may be. It takes time to heal and time to know yourself well enough to know how to move forward. Anxiety is something that comes in waves, I do not know if there is a solution, you just get better at handling it so you can function and even thrive. -Sophie

I would describe your illness as a nightmare which requires a large amount of self-control and discipline so that it doesn't take over your life. The problem is trauma and addiction in my opinion. I think you have been very good about handling the addiction component of the disorder as you've made very conscious and measurable steps to mitigate those. Trauma on the other hand is something whose solution is hard to grasp. This will take time and personal healing more than anything else. Although others can help you through this, I believe you have to find the solution yourself. −Paul

Sometimes I think the "problem," if that's how it should be described, is that…media forms like popular books, TV shows, and movies—and even our peers—

tell us we should enjoy sexual encounters, that sex is
fun, or that we are lucky when someone wants to have
sex with us, without underlining that safe and
respectful and consensual sex is what is important, not
just the sex act alone. So that can confuse or distort
our perception, so we think a traumatic and
disrespectful or unwanted sexual encounter is okay
because sex means someone wants us, even if it hurts
us. And part of me wonders if this is why Austin found
himself in so many triggering situations—because on
some level the pop culture of our society told us it was
okay, wanted even. Because the pop culture of our
society romanticized rape culture and even if you can
recognize it is wrong and rationalize that you don't
enjoy it, it's difficult to take that stand for yourself,
especially if it defies society's norms… -Shannon

You don't trust yourself and you let your fears
overwhelm you. You're stuck on what used to be and
have trouble moving on. -Krysti

the chorus reacts:

I felt the enormity of what Austin entrusted to me, and
felt the trust and vulnerability he was sharing with me.
His testimony made me appreciate the fragility of
Austin's day to day life. My perception changed, I
respected his resolve to move forward, and was more

inclined to view his actions with sympathy because he carries a great burden. Given the nature of our friendship, I do not think his illness changed our interactions, if anything it made us closer because it opened the door to more open dialogue. I think the biggest challenge to being a part of his healing process was knowing what to say. I was afraid of making Austin feel worse. -Sophie

After Austin shared his experiences with me, I was frustrated. I was upset that he'd been put in that situation and that he now had to cope with the effects of an event that was for someone else's gain and that hurt him. Part of me couldn't understand why he had continued to be unable to escape or stop events that continued to hurt them—I couldn't understand the repetition of these situations in his life—but then I realized I do the same thing with other things in my life, in another way, and how you can become addicted to that pattern, even when you know it's wrong…Austin's testimony made me understand him better and made me more aware of what matters to him or what might resonate with him. It also made me realize how strong he was, for living through traumatic event after traumatic event and having a positive outlook and hope for new friends (like I was) or romantic relationships despite the people who had hurt him. It makes me really proud of him that he didn't give up…and instead found ways to cope and found healthy outlets for what he was dealing with. I don't know, I don't think about it all the time, but it's pretty impressive. It's also a stupid, stubborn thing, but I'm also impressed that he stayed at Wake and didn't transfer or take a semester off for mental health or whatever. It shows me how determined he is that he didn't let what happened on this campus or during his time in college keep him from going after his goals, and attaining them. To me, that's the best kick in the balls he could give to those who tried to victimize him. I think Austin's illness has affected how I interact with him in that I'm more aware of where he's coming from or of possible reasons for him doing things that may frustrate me. I think sometimes my biggest challenge in being part of Austin's healing process has been feeling like sometimes my advice or attempts to talk through some fear or worry he has is taken for granted—either because I don't or can't fully understand what he's been through or where he's coming from (so what advice can I really offer and why should he take it seriously?)…My other, stronger fear is that if something very upsetting were to happen, like a break-up that didn't end well or a strong strain in a relationship, Austin may turn back to the pattern of traumatic situations in his history… I don't want him to become so upset he thinks he deserves to be hurt or doesn't deserve to be respected and loved. –Shannon

I felt sad and helpless. I couldn't do anything but listen. I had no solution. There was nothing I could say to make you feel better and I was/am afraid to say the wrong thing and make you feel worse. Yes, I find myself unable to comfort you. I still don't know what to say or do. When I hear from you and you're having an extra difficult day, I don't know how to act or how to help, so I change the subject or ignore it. The hardest part was not knowing how to help you and getting frustrated when you have so many good things going for you but you can't get past the bad. I was afraid that you wouldn't recover, and I'm still worried about the panic/anxiety attacks that you have. -Krysti

Well, immediately I was scared and confused. I didn't know how to treat you after knowledge of your experiences. I honestly didn't have words, but after processing time I began to start to understand it. Although I have never experienced the same things in my life, to a degree I can relate to the mentally derailing portion of your illness. I began to realize that you had more control over yourself that I had initially seen, which made me much more comfortable speaking with you and walking with you through this process. And yes, I have changed the way I interact with you based on your illness, especially since we are in an intimate relationship. Some might have found it difficult to evolve to the needs of another and to empathize with their feelings, but that's love to me. I was able to see how some of my words/actions/opinions might affect you and have used that to not only help you grow, but to help myself learn. -Paul

I suppose after that I might have felt mildly protective over you. Or maybe I bent my antenna a little more strongly your way, but otherwise, no big change. It just made me feel closer to you. It was definitely hard not knowing the extent to which I could ask questions, follow up, check in on you. I'm not pushy, and everyone has varying space needs, so as much as it ran counter to my wishes, I let you have your space. Unsure how much intrusion you wanted, I consciously backed off more than once. -Alyssa

It's always hard when you love someone who is struggling. The hardest parts for me were being patient when he didn't want to talk about something or share what was going on. –Meredith

the chorus ponders:

I think Austin's biggest obstacle is self-care. I think he is too hard on himself and often times overlooks what would soothe him. -Sophie

The biggest challenge for me are the moments of no communication. I still do not understand that part of your illness and probably never will, but it is something I have learned to accept and work through. I tend to get very frustrated with you when you can't tell me what's wrong or what's going on with you knowing that in a few hours you would be able to speak about it. I have learned to let go of control of this situation and leave you to handle things yourself, calling on me when you need me the most. That isn't how I would have ever approached things, as I deal with things immediately, but now I understand that it can't always happen that way. I see you as your biggest obstacle, because of the nature of your illness which has become a part of you. (thinking of Harry having to get rid of the horcrux within himself to truly be his own self) You are very comfortable with your daily schedule and routine, even though this illness follows you through every step. I see you breaking through this illness when you are able to break through yourself as an individual. -Paul

Sometimes I think Austin's biggest obstacle may be choosing what's best for him, even if the people he loves want something else from him at the time. I don't think Austin wants to upset the people he cares about or make them angry and sometimes I worry this results in him putting himself in situations he doesn't really want to be in or not to take care of himself (though I think he's become increasingly stronger at surmounting this obstacle). -Shannon

I think your biggest obstacle is being able to trust yourself and be in an independent relationship – I worry about what will happen if Paul moves. -Krysti

I've always had total faith in Austin. No fears or uncertainties. But the biggest obstacle? Probably the thing that is hardest for all of us—complete and total self-acceptance and love. -Meredith

the chorus advises:

My advice: Don't beat yourself up so much. -Sophie

Use your experiences to help others. I know you're going to already, because you're going to be a doctor. Love you! -Meredith

My advice is to trust yourself and don't worry as much about what people think. Spend some time alone, take some time to heal. -Krysti

Continue to work hard on yourself and always stay the charming/beautiful person you are. Be open to change and be willing to take off your lens to look through the lens of another, even in the most difficult of circumstances. -Paul

One piece of advice: you have to live the way that makes you happiest, or the way that you will be at peace with. And you have to live for yourself and not someone else, and don't worry about what may happen between you and the people you care about. The people who really matter in your life will be there at the end of the day, it's all serendipity—it all works out the way it's supposed to. (At least, serendipity is the greatest advice I was ever given). Also, I love you. -Shannon

commencement

These may be the hardest questions of all. *What do you want for your future? What does recovery look like for you?* I've been asked these questions so many times, and I never really have a full answer because I honestly do not know. I want to feel at peace. I want to feel equipped and able to handle the waves of anxiety that will come, and I want to ride those waves and watch them pass rather than being knocked over by them. I want to be free of flashbacks. I don't want to forget all that happened; I used to think it would be better if I did, but without those memories I would not understand how I survived to become the person I am today. I still want to believe in the kindness of strangers, and that people are inherently good. Those two are hard for me. I want to trust people, to not be paranoid that people will leave after they see all that has been and is within me. I want to reduce how much medication I'm on. I just want to be me.

2 june 2016

The anxiety that I bitterly fought against last winter/spring is back. It instills itself in my chest and throat, where I feel its every breath and move. I feel it in my heart beat, which becomes stronger and more rapid and more exhausting. I feel it in the suffocating pressure that lodges itself in my throat. I feel it in my upset stomach. It's with me when I wake up in the morning but thankfully goes away sometime in the afternoon. Yesterday I felt it begin to loosen its grip around lunch, which was earlier than usual. I can't beat it with my medicine in the morning because I usually wake up with it in my chest already. I'm not exactly sure what its root cause is. My best guess would be my living alone in Chapel Hill. I'm absolutely terrified of being alone. It's not something I'm comfortable with yet and I don't trust myself to be alone, not after all the episodes. I guess it's right that my body is so keyed up when I'm alone because it's expecting something bad to happen. But I'm in a different place, a different time, and a different situation. Those experiences won't happen again-- I am safe. But my body doesn't quite believe that, not yet. I'm uncomfortable with the amount of free time I have right now, where I'm left with myself. It's also hard to live with one foot in Chapel Hill and one in Winston-Salem. I keep living in terms of getting through the days where I'm not in Winston, where I'm not coming home to Paul. I don't like how I frame my days in this manner. Right now though, maybe it's how I need to get by. I want to be able to enjoy the day for what it is, rather than what's to come in the future. It's much less stressful and would help me to be more present and to feel more alive. This will take time, I know.

what once was, now is, once again (june 23 2016)

She called me three times night before last around 1
AM; I didn't think much about it at the time because
that's when she gets off work and I assumed she just
wanted to talk. I texted her yesterday and she said she
was okay so I moved on. I just got a text from her
saying that she'd been sexually assaulted that night. I
feel sick, hazy, sore, stiff. My lungs feel calcified. The
places that hurt for me now hurt for her. But I haven't
cried; why can't I cry?

cold water

I feel the rush of water down my back
The cascade of chills and shudders arch my spine
I close my eyes after they've opened too wide
And my focus shifts to a sinusoidal recurrence
Bronchoconstriction without termination

The mirage expands in site and cast
And you're in it now, before the worst has passed
But you're not here, you're far away
But I think you'll stay, you'll stay
But I don't act that way, no not that way
I try to make you say, but you can't say
That there will be better days
Maybe tomorrow will be a better day

After the rain pours the rivers flood
Rushing waters obscure the gentle curves of the sandy
cove
The cattails fall down, reeds broken asymmetrically, to
merciless waves
Bugs scatter but can't run away
Water fast and deep, liquid obsidian from a frostbit
kingdom

And it starts to trickle, my spine prickles
And I feel what's coming, the thoracic rock sinks down
a bit further
My hands wring and my heart beats heavier

i looked under the bed and didn't see a monster (6 july 2016)

I went to Winston last night and while at the bar Paul & I began talking about the fluidity in his sexuality and about one of the reasons he wants to have sex outside of our relationship: he doesn't want to hurt or trigger me with some of his sexual desires and fantasies. Knowing this has made the prospect of him being with other men less scary. I can trust him, I can trust him, I can trust him and I believe him. I'm still scared of sex, of being violated, or having my trust betrayed, of a lot of things. But this conversation softened a few of those fears. We talked for a long time and both cried together under the rain shower head, the lukewarm water diluting our tears and sending chills down my spine as it cooled. Paul cried from the relief of being free from the weight of that truth and I cried because I realized that I can and do trust him. I realized that I am able trust someone deeply again.

the beast

The beast has arrived
But without cacophonous revelation
It's not huge, nor fanged, nor hairy, nor clawed

It's insidious
It's quiet
It crept up on me, leaving its subtle traces along the
way

I didn't realize what these things meant until today

i'm a medical student now (4 august 2016)

It's been a while since I've sat down to write. Several weeks, to be exact. So much has happened and I don't know where to begin with everything I want to process. I'm writing as I wait for lecture to start, sitting in the front row of the lecture hall. It's still surreal that I'm in medical school. It doesn't feel "real" just yet. It feels a bit odd, a bit disjointed from what I expected. But I guess that's the point of adjustment. I'm a bit nervous about whether I'll make good friends here or if I'll stay on a professional periphery with my classmates. I just haven't felt like I've really "clicked" with anyone just yet. I recognize that friendships take time to cultivate and develop, but I wish I'd found something genuine and a bit more instantaneous. Maybe I'm just being whiny. I need to remember why I'm here: to become a physician. I'm here for myself, not for anyone else.

I've been struggling with the idea that I'm an imposter, or a fraud. The Sunday before orientation started, I remember crying consistently throughout the day because I was scared that something inside me would crack from the pressure of being found a fraud. I guess I still don't believe that I deserve to be here. I haven't felt like I belong here: not academically or socially. I think it's the exhaustion of this major transition and the fact that I tend to incessantly criticize myself. But there's something deeper for which I can't account.

Last Sunday was hard, regardless of the impending start of medical school. Paul's friend (an acquaintance of mine) committed suicide the Wednesday before and we attended the funeral that afternoon. It left me feeling sad and unsettled and I almost felt like I didn't have the right to feel as deep a loss as I did.

insidious

2 miles away

The blue and orange messages that bounce between our virtual selves

When the portal is closed, the guilt sets in

But when you turn back around, resistance dims

Incapacitated, conflicted, pleading for an Irish exit

But your fingers type out monologues that you can't support

Somehow, though, they're set free

And the cycle continues onwards

Gathering speed and taking its toll

25 feet away

The pressure builds from core to throat

Asphyxiating, hypnotizing, commandeering control

I'm observing the cascade, the submission, the fall

From a prison locked away

Desire, a drug I can't inject

A sacrifice tomorrow won't justify

I follow the lines to let you in

Names aren't important here

Emotions take heed to the force above us

A carnal canvas, physical expressions of frustration

Repression drove us into the dark places

after the relapse (15 august 2016)

I had my first exam of medical school today. I did well,
that's what I want to remind myself. Bernie introduced
a helpful image in therapy: a boulder perched on top of
a great hill. The boulder rolling into the valley
represents the thing that you don't want to happen,
and he talked about how I could think about putting
obstacles on the slope to help the boulder from
reaching the valley. My boulder in the valley is an
episode or flashback, or at the moment, being with
anyone else sexually besides Paul. I don't think I'm
ready for that. We talked about what puts the boulder
on top of the hill: an emotional event that serves as a
stimulus and gives the boulder a push to start it rolling
down the hill. The habit is a response to a feeling of
exhaustion partnered with frustration, boredom, and
self-loathing. I felt so much pressure during
orientation to make new friends and I felt a bit
worthless and out of place during that time. Imposter
syndrome may have led my mind to find relief in
seeking out strangers who would glorify my body as a
manner of tending to the growing hurt and pain inside
me that I hadn't found a way to digest. Sexuality had
also been on my mind a lot as I'd been meeting the gay
men in my class and I've been afraid of gay men for so
long that they can automatically represent predators

that I perceive as orchestrating another episode. After seeing what could have pushed my boulder close to the edge, I began to think about what roadblocks / obstacles I can establish on the slope in order to prevent it from defeating me. I've thought to find a way to reach out to Paul when I'm feeling these emotions and in situations where I could slip into the hijacked consciousness, and spending time doing things that make me proud of myself and make me feel good about myself: having a good swim, working in a coffee shop, writing, and spending time with friends. I need some time to come down from the rush of this session and to be able to process everything. I want to be proud that I stopped the episode from becoming anything more consuming than it was; I was able to take some control back for myself. I ended up telling Paul about the episode. I was terrified that what I had to say would tarnish or ruin our relationship. As I sobbed on his bed, in his arms, he told me it would never ruin our relationship. He said that even if it had been a conscious choice, it would not have been the end for him. I felt deeply ashamed and embarrassed at what had happened but I am so, so lucky that Paul is who he is. I want to get better for myself, but I also want to get better for him. I recognize that my history and current situation must be incredibly hard for him to understand and work with, and I want him to be able to enjoy his own life and mine without all that's currently going on. Sobriety is difficult and it's challenging. Staying "clean" is something that I will have to confront every day for the rest of my life, if it's something I want to commit to for the rest of my life. I'll start with just tackling my homework and my day tomorrow. Then I'll look to confront Thursday. Then the next day, and the next and the next. I am strong, I can do this. I can do it. I'll end with a happy note. The Iron & Wine concert this past Saturday was magical. I'd kept it a surprise from Paul until we'd found seats on the lawn of the amphitheater at the NC Museum of Art. The music was entrancing, just how I'd imagined it. Drunk off a bottle of Chardonnay and with my favorite person, it was by far the highlight of my summer, I believe. I want to have more days and nights where I feel as light, as happy, as liberated, as capable as I did that night. I wasn't weighed down by my consciousness of reality and of the blurriness constructing my future. I was present, I was part of something greater than myself, and I was in a state where I could deeply appreciate and take in the beauty of what was going on around me. That's what I want for my life. That's who I want to be.

re: *the hunting ground*, a documentary

I don't really remember what all happened when I decided to tell someone.

It was after the time in the rain, the cold April rain, when he didn't ask before he did it.

I don't remember who I first told.

I remember being shuttled to the office in the back corner of the administrative building.

How I wasn't encouraged to report it. I don't remember what I was offered.

And now I'm realizing in retrospect that I would have had to live with the guy who hurt me sophomore year if the room across campus hadn't opened up.

But this time that I asked for help—since it wasn't on campus, there wasn't much they could do.

I think that these things still haunt me.

I think it's why sex cannot be wholly good, not yet. There is still something dark about it.

There's a reason why I always want him to finish quickly. How it only truly feels good every so often.

I remember the woman I met with in the "Safe" office, who I was convinced was kind and of the utmost support.

But now, years later, I don't feel supported.

I feel very alone. I don't know how to feel better, necessarily. I don't know when all these things started and which ones should "count" and if my own volition is responsible for others. It's simultaneously all too much and not enough.

There's a reason I sometimes dream of shoving an icicle through my temples. I won't admit to it but it's a common companion in my mind.

There's still that huge part of me that does not believe myself. That part is convinced that I am making these claims up, that this is all an elaborate fabrication to soothe an attention-seeking cyst inside me.

There's also a piece of me that wants to believe it all. That wants to acknowledge that something, something did happen.

What it was exactly I don't know, maybe I never will.

I just don't know what to think. I feel like I've been holding my breath for too long. Maybe that indicates that I've arrived at some form of truth.

22 august 2016

After last weekend, I knew I needed a debrief to help me process. I told Bernie everything that happened in between our meeting last Monday and today; from confessing the episode to Paul to the week of frustration and building spite to the weekend where I noticed a crumbling, then a cracking, then a dissolution of the façade I'd built upon over these few weeks. I regressed into myself, a darker, once-toxic place that conjured striking, frightening feelings reminiscent of times where I'd really lost control over the person I was and who I was becoming: the end of my NCSSM career and the first part of my Wake Forest career. This past weekend left me feeling broken, drained, silly, exhausted, alone, childish, and scared. None of which helped me to see what I've done and what I'm doing currently. I'm pursuing my professional dream: attending medical school to become a physician. I'm also learning to take care of myself, for the first time in my life. It's not a straightforward process, contrary to what I'd quietly hoped.

We also established a more detailed, flush image of what drives my panic attacks. My worst-case scenario is simple: I've lost. I've been defeated by the episodes, the PTSD, the sex addiction, the trauma, the anxiety of not being able to control the future, and the bulimia. I've been abandoned by the one person to whom I've borne everything and I've had my trust and love discarded, violated and used. I've been isolated and I'm totally and eternally alone. That's my worst-case scenario. It's oddly comforting to be able to see it now. It's bleak and it's not particularly pleasant to entertain but just how naming a disease can bring relief, visualizing my most fundamental fear has some therapeutic value. Now the work comes in the form of relieving the panic attacks that this shifting, unpinned, amorphous presence can precipitate. I tried positive, rationalizing self-talk last night when I felt the panic. It didn't necessarily "work" but it's a good start to an arsenal of tools I can utilize in order to beat back the advancing front.

I can feel a difference in me, from who I was a few years (or even just a few months) ago to the person that I am now. I don't think I have the right combination of words or the most illustrious narrative to describe that shift, but I can see it, even if it's just a glimpse. Maybe it's a glimpse of the "real adult" I want to become, the optimal version of myself that I've been longing for. Bernie helped me to put words to this self, something I've not been able to do until today. It's very simple: confidence. My self-confidence and self-esteem can be remarkably lacking at times; when Bernie asked me what this version of myself looked and felt like, it was a me that was able to carry myself with confidence effortlessly. It was an incarnation of me that held a deeply rooted belief, a resounding truth, that I will be okay, that I am okay. It's a me that's proud of what I've done and what I will do in the future. It's a me that believes in my potential to do great things, a version of myself that believes that I'm gifted and able to become an incredibly skillful, competent, astute and sensitive clinician. It's someone who's in good physical shape, who follows his dream of becoming a writer (in some capacity), who nurtures deep friendships, and who holds dear to his partner. I can see myself being that person in medical school. I'm here, in the midst of that image that came to mind when Bernie asked me that question. I can do it. I can.

Bernie left me with a question to ponder: what will I do, the "other thing" when I experience the challenging periods where my resolve, composure, and strength are tested? This period is transformative in appearance, whether it be a panic attack, a surge of a potential episode, or a period where I'm very much on my own. What will I do to divert the trajectory from crashing into a place I'd rather not revisit? I don't fully know the answer to this question.

2-4 september 2016

It's one of those moments where I have access to a
crevice extending from my core to some undisclosed
location in a different dimension. I am confident, I am
present, I am full. I believe in who I am, in what I'm
doing, in what I'm not. There are twinges of pain in
my temples and my foot is engaged in a familiar
constant shaking. I feel as though I could stare
through the brick wall across from me if I rearranged
the electrical circuit of my nervous system just right.
I'm sitting at a table on the fourth floor of Berryhill
before Pathology lab, looking out over the hospital to
the south and the serrated horizon lines of forest and
clouds. There's a hurricane on the way today. The sky
is that captivating swath of grey-white uniformity, the
sky that I associate with England, where I would lay in
my bed and look out my bedroom and could
perceptively witness myself falling in love with
something much greater than myself. I think that's
happening here. I realized yesterday that I think I'm
happy here. I'm proud of myself for making this
transition; a transition into someone who society
perceives as sacrificing everything in order to
contribute to a greater good. There's a bit of
sacrilegious satisfaction in knowing that I will not, and
have not, made that sacrifice. I almost feel like a con

artist as a medical student. People see me as being much greater than I actually am, and I won't try to change their minds. I know what my core is composed of and I acknowledge the disparity as an old friend. The inside doesn't match the outside, but I'm okay with that. I feel the scattered pieces of myself starting to draw back together, a low-level magnetic force that's pulling everything back into my core.

I'm proud of myself for what I did this week. I lived through anxiety attacks. I saw the impending wave, I felt the sand and water pulled from under my feet as the tsunami towered above me. Instead of drowning I closed my eyes and felt it crashing down on top of me but found a way to keep at least one foot planted on the ground. I did it. Me. Myself. I.

I passed my first block of medical school. I can do this. I will be a physician. It's beginning to become a digestible image that I can start to believe, I think. The standardized patient I worked with on Tuesday told me that the exam I gave was indicative that I was meant to be in medicine. I'm relieved that my presence is something that feels comfortable to patients. I was, and am, really proud of that. Even if I barely completed the physical exam, I'm proud of who I was during the experience. It felt like the foundation of something great.

You close your eyes for just a moment, just to rest your eyes for a few breaths. But then when you open your eyes and nothing is familiar, your insides calcify and you're at the mercy by the fear of not recognizing what is in and around you. I didn't recognize what was brewing inside me, and I was terrified of what would slip out of my body, in small trails of smoke, polluting the air around me.

I've never called myself a jealous person. I also would have never called myself gay, agnostic, anxious, depressed, or happy, once upon a time.

I found a beautiful cove, shaded from the brawl of storms and piracy and urban development. The flora and fauna undisturbed, the sand following pristine waves across the shore. The seashells haven't been obliterated by off-shore dredging, the crabs migrate across the crescent beach in groups that scuttle without fear of being trampled, and the birds sing songs of love, flight, and celebration. The breeze is gentle, but ever changing, challenging the life of the cove to constantly change and grow in response.

But I cherish this cove to the point where I'm terrified that it will be stampeded by invaders, whose identities can change at any time. I'm terrified that I will lose my presence and my place there, that what I find precious will be stolen away from me. It is not my right to claim this cove as my own, but I want to, because it's safe to do something along those lines. It's comforting to feel in control, to feel as though nothing can intercept your experience of being here in this cove. I have no intelligence or warnings of imminent invaders except those stemming from my own imagination. But those are just as frightening as any other.

The winds that batter the boat change just as quickly as they are recognized. I am so happy in this moment. I just lost a play fight that involved two slices of muddled cucumber, an umbrella utilized as a battering ram, and the realization that I am with the person I want to be my partner in life.

I overcame this afternoon's jealousy and accompanying anxiety. I did it. I fought through it and survived and kept my own darkness contained. It passed, and I can breathe. I know it will come again but I can deal with it, I can control it.

I am happy.

And once again, the tides have redistributed themselves along the ocean's edge to create a different shore; the water has shifted and collected along different gullies, it leaves others exposed, the carcasses of shellfish and small sea life that couldn't stay with the current exposed to the salty air.

I feel remorse for what I've been dealing with when in reality, I have really no blame for the emotions and feelings that rise up within me like lava that's finally found a weak spot in the Earth's crust. My mood and physical feelings follow the predetermined course of a sinusoidal curve, I fear. Up and down and up and down, not static but always bending ever so slightly to a new local maximum or minimum. Predictable yet exhausting.

At least I can see it, I can put words to it, I can identify what I'm fighting to disassemble and process. That's an early step. I look at the section above and see what a healed me will look like. The stars are invisible during the day, when the sunlight obliterates them from the naked eye, but they always shine through at night. They always do.

rewritten as a dream

My eyes closed // Your hands press deep into my flesh // I feel your fingertips between the muscles of my back // a prophet parting the sea // the towel rubs indentations into my face // I can smell the lavender oil on your hands // the air is cold on my bare skin // my stomach is hidden // no need to suck in right now

Your lips are a fruit too fragile to bite // your lisp curls around the gap between two of your bottom teeth // your hair falls from behind your ears and tickles my cheekbones // Eyes reflecting the blue-greys of a winter's sea // You touch my cheek and I fall into a deeper place of which I used to dream

But I feel myself slipping away // into a reserved enclosure inside my head // spectator, not participant, now I assume // I feel the touch, I feel the tension, I feel the anxious contraction // I beg to scream // *this is not your fault this is not your fault* // but my lips fail to break a wax-pressed seal // frustration builds as my body is moved as a marionette // my mind begins to accept defeat

I see that the face above me isn't yours // but rather that I found solace in a crime // hold tight // move fast // don't breathe // it'll be over soon

I don't forget // that I pretended that it was you.

hold it in until it's safe to break (8 september 2016)

There are times where giving up is tempting, where it almost seems logical. I woke up feeling defeated; I woke up with the pressure and constriction of anxiety in my throat and chest after getting a full night's sleep. I started the day with the feeling that I'd already conceded the victory to the opponent and that did not set me up to have a day where I felt in control of myself, or of my life. The amount of anxiety I felt and carried on me yesterday was draining and almost overwhelming; getting through the day was the best I could do. I'm starting to feel a bit anxious now, as I write this reflection, and I feel like it's residual from yesterday as well as something more continuous, more ingrained to the contours of my physicality.

Yesterday's session with Bernie was one of the more difficult ones. I immediately burst into tears when I sat down and I could tell he was concerned. We did some EMDR processing work around feeling unsafe/distressed/anxious when I'm alone in my apartment and I felt a lot better after the appointment yesterday; but the feeling came back a few hours later. I felt like I was being torn apart from my core. I was rattled by fear, anxiety, and hurt. I felt rejected and alone. When I met Paul at the bar downstairs in his building I felt calm, relaxed, and happy. I felt safe and I felt secure. But then, when we started watching tennis for the rest of the evening, the anxiety crept back. It focused on his texting his friend who is gay and somewhat resembles me physically. I'm terrified that there's a sexual or emotional connection between them that extends beyond a platonic friendship.

I know that my issues have had negative effects on Paul and I don't want him to leave me because of what I'm dealing with. I'm terrified that he will. I'm terrified of gay men because of how deeply sex is engrained in our identities; when I see a gay man, that's the first thing that comes to my mind. I wish that were different.

I'm writing this on a bench outside of Bondurant under the trees on the side walkway. I feel like I could cry right now, or fall asleep, or just melt into nothingness. I am looking forward to going home tonight; it will nice to be able to be with Mom and to have her comforting presence around me.

I just want to be better. I want to be able to live my life here independently and comfortably. I don't want to feel hijacked by a parasitic presence any longer.

I want to feel capable of confronting loneliness and anxiety and to be able to process it and move on. I don't want to feel dependent on being with other people in order to feel happy or safe. I want to be healed, conclusively.

the chief complaint

He is anxious. Or rather, he has anxiety. He is afraid of
a complete reversal, one where he's pulled back into
the world he's worked so hard to escape. He wakes up
with a tightness in the base of his throat, a tightness
that can crawl through his chest, into his shoulders,
and into his lungs. He finds that he's not breathing
more often than not. His heart beats perceptively; he
feels every beat with the magnitude of a great
stampede. A rope pulls his temples together, tugging
his insides from down within a deep crevice of his
torso; if he allowed his body to follow the trajectory,
he would fold in upon himself, a black hole in its final
moments. He is afraid. He is afraid of the reemergence
of the depression that plagued sophomore year. He is
afraid of the day when the four-drug cocktail finally
fails to deliver. He's afraid of people misunderstanding
him, of not really understanding it himself. He's afraid
of defeat, of being conquered a final, ultimate time. He
is afraid of what they did, that somehow it can't be
fixed. Il a peur de ces hommes. Leurs visages sont
cimentés dans les vestiges kaléidoscopiques qui se sont
collés à l'intérieur de ses paupières. Cette mosaïque est
un cauchemar qui transcende le sommeil ; il transcende
la mémoire, le temps, la réalité. He is afraid of people,
because he fears that he can no longer engage with

them in the world outside of an internal cacophony. He is afraid of loss, of losing the most intimate relationships and friendships that he has been able to carry with him to this moment. He is afraid of what people will think of the past and current lists of diagnoses: *anxiety/post-traumatic stress disorder/trauma-induced sex addiction/bulimia nervosa*. He is proud of what he was able to do despite the sky raining kerosene above a field of matches. But he is afraid that the sky will catch fire, that the night sky will be consumed by flames. He worries, somedays more than others. There are good days, ones where he only takes one pill. But there are the days where he can barely keep his body from flying apart into a million unresolvable shards. He is sometimes afraid that the promises he made to himself in black ink across his body won't form a strong enough anchor for those days. But somehow, he is here, he is no longer in the past, today he is here. But something still lingers, an elusive, trailing, tempting, striking, constricting, faceless, boundless entity whose echoes you can hear if you know when to listen. He's getting better, he's much better, he can see what it would be like to be healed, to be a derivative of an idealized whole self that sits at the base of the altar littered by his body's dutiful sacrifices. But he worries. His body has erected a magnificently intricate and damning defense system to prepare for the worst-case scenarios that sometimes play in an ever-intensifying loop in his head. He worries because his body has taken the brunt of the fall and can't relax, not just yet.

He is anxious.

for the times when I fell back into the cycle

You won't come home
No not yet
You don't come home
Not what I expect
You say that a friend is in town
Just for the day
You say you're going to meet for drinks
Just after work
You're not home when I open the door
At the end of the day
I don't turn on the light
In the fading light
I let the sun set while I lay down
For a little rest
Maybe this is all an overreaction
Yeah, that's it
A projection of a conscience lacking retribution
An unpaid debt
The things I didn't tell you in times apart
The necessary last hits
A story I can never fully tell
The ending isn't set

You aren't home
No not yet

I wonder who he is
If this is it
I hope he can fill in the craters of the broken parts I
can't give
Yes, that's it
The parts of me that can't find solace in unity
Failed before we even met

I won't ask
You don't tell
I won't worry
You can't tell
I don't judge
You won't as well.

turn your gaze upwards

The sky is blue. A resounding Carolina blue. The color is rich and permeates the horizon: above, behind, down, around. Lying on your back, staring directly upwards at an unbounded atmospheric display, there is nothing else. A bird may fly across your field of vision, buoyant in the currents that direct the wind across landscapes. A white, pillowing cloud may float across your field of vision. It's an interruption in the maritime peace that bring solace to your eyes, but it's only a momentary distraction. There, in another corner of your periphery, another cloud arrives. This one isn't pure white like the first; there are smudges of grey. This cloud is reminiscent of smudges made by an artist adding depth to a pencil drawing, or watery remains of a forehead on Ash Wednesday. There's a mystery embedded in the soft transition from white to grey, one that's entrancing. You close your eyes after you meet these clouds with a steady gaze. You don't feel threatened, it's just two clouds.

Time passes almost imperceptibly and when you open your eyes the scene is unrecognizable. Swirling tufts of heavy, dark clouds threaten to transform into a maelstrom before your eyes; the weight of the darkness brings the sky much closer, where you inhale a bit of the sagging moisture with every breath. It's silent, it's threatening, and the sky may crack open into a storm that tears you into jagged, soaked pieces that don't offer an obvious reassembly.

But if you can remember that the clouds move, that rain will fall in gentle and torrential cascades, that clouds fade away into the night sky, you can survive this if you dig your hands and heels into the cold earth. You can look past them, through the miles of swaths of grey and black fog and you can see the blue sky above it, the blue sky that is obscured by the brewing storm. The blue sky still exists just beyond what's visible. The blue sky that can be seen again.

Hold on to the grass below your body, hug your sweater and blankets close to hold in the warmth, and recite poetry to the rhythm of a morning glory on the verge of its daily blossoming. Wait, hold fast, and wait. You will see the sky once again.

14 september 2016

Looking back at my composure a week ago, I feel like a
completely different person. The feeling of losing grip
is absent; I just feel tense, tired, and a tad unsettled.
The session with Bernie today was really productive,
in a way that left me feeling more whole than when I
entered the room at the beginning. We talked a lot
about the force that pulls and tightens within me, the
one that instructs my body to fold in upon itself and to
become seamless with the invisible layers of another
dimension. We talked about what phrase we used in
last week's EMDR processing, "I can't take care of
myself", and how the negative statement is meant to be
reflective of an irrational fear. But it's not irrational in
these bursts of anxiety and consuming physical
defense; I'm searching for a way to take care of myself
and have been unsuccessful thus far. We arrived at
possibly a more appropriate phrase: I am powerless.
That one resonates more deeply, it rattles me in ways
that evoke fear and sadness. I have felt utterly
powerless, so many times before: when I lost Grandma
to cancer, when I was caught between my burgeoning
identity and sexuality and my family's belief system,
when I went to NCSSM, when I went to Wake Forest,
when I began having episodes, when I felt that the line
of consent was crossed and I could not speak up

regardless of the voice screaming inside me, when I went abroad to London, when I began applying to medical school, when I found myself accepting my spot at UNC, when I moved to Chapel Hill. It's as if my body has solely been conditioned to feel loss, and nothing else. I've often berated myself for not feeling excited, not feeling grateful for what privileges I have in my life. But I guess my body just doesn't have the mechanism solidified for experiencing these things. Bernie used a few phrases that have really resonated with me: I don't know where to put my power when I'm in situations where I have the opportunity (i.e. a free afternoon and I can't even decide or identify what I would want to do) and that I struggle to find ways to assert a claim to my life. Now that I have the words, I can finally imagine how assertion could manifest itself in my future.

l'éveil (28 december 2016)

These violent ends have violent delights.

When I picture the self that began this journal and contrast him with the self who breathes and aches and thinks in the ever-present moment, I sense the shadow of a radical shift. I sense the movement away from a place of indebted submission to an idea that was never true, but its strength was in the fallacy of its essence: *you can be a bad person. You are a bad person, Austin. You are not good. You are not enough. You are not powerful. You are not in control.*

What I needed to break the cycle wasn't solely medication or therapy. It was time. I needed time to suffer just long enough at my own hand in order to understand what it was that I sought to confront. I confronted myself. It didn't happen in a single moment, but rather in a growing crescendo continuum. I bitterly fought against the revolution of falling into my own self not in implosion but in creation. I'm finally creating my own self, the person that *I want to be*. Not the person that I'm expected to be, or taught to be, or guided to be, or anything apart from a personhood envisioned and imagined by my own consciousness.

I declared independence. I tied the loose ends to make knots. I wrote endings to stories whose last chapters were painstakingly prolonged. I made peace with myself, at a minute level at its commencement, which enlightened me to the direction of the center of myself. I didn't have the imagery during the moments that I first felt this, but I often felt as I was moving along a predetermined trajectory, an exquisite mannequin acting out a fantasy built upon the millions of fragments that compose my human experience.

I feel free. It's not a joyous feeling. Rather, it feels as though the fragment of rock that broke away from the jagged cliff and fell to the river below, that fragment has been smoothed over decades into a sleek stone. Cold to the touch, an infinite surface with no boundaries or borders. I'll never see every speck that composes this infinity, but I want to discover as many as I can in my future.

But, with the birth of an avant-garde comes the death of the predecessor. The me who ended, the me that met its demise. That person is fading down, a decrescendo into memory, into preservation and containment. This me felt out of control, victimized, overwhelmed, and at the mercy of others in order to create happiness. *I do not believe that I am this person any longer.*

I am finally in accordance with what I tattooed on my inner forearm: *I am free. Je suis libre. Je suis libre. Je suis libre.*

I'm nervous of the future that 2017 may bring. The moving components of the world around me are menacing, threatening to revisit dark places from humankind's past. But I will write beautiful stories of my own, in order to remind myself that *I am not the world around me. I am myself, first and always.* I will marry Paul in a few weeks. I will continue to refine my professional self, to continue to mold myself into the physician I envision being. I will continue to make the small choices that will advance my progression deeper into the labyrinth of myself, to discover just what lies in my core, in my dead center. I will take care of my body, of my mind, of *my inner self.* I will do this because it is why I am alive, for the purpose of why I am free. I am my own meaning. Now I can go forth and reach ethereal heights.

atonement for the flesh

The first line
This is for you
The little boy that Mommy said was sweet, was special, was soft
The little boy that played with Barbies when no one was looking
Putting them in the most flattering clothes, brushing their hair, saying *you are beautiful*
The little boy that pretended
That he too could fit in with the little girls
The girl toys were always more fun, anyway
But this was a secret, a secret, don't let Daddy know, can't let him know
Mommy knows but it's a secret kept between the two of you
He's sweet and sensitive, he's a sweet little boy

This is for you
The little boy who drew maps
Of continents existing only in his mind
City maps laid out in neat grids
School districts and hospitals were planned
Street names chosen with particularly careful consideration

This is for you
The second line
This one cut a little bit deeper
This is for you
The boy that annually lost friends he had tried so hard
to keep
The boy that bounced from group to group
Waiting for another iteration of middle school drama
To force him out
To prove that *yes, you are not worthy*
You must try harder because you are not good enough
No one cared that you were smart
That you knew the capitals of countries adults don't
recognize
That you did solo special projects for social studies
classes in which you'd placed out
That you have your books (lunchtime companions)
lined up in neat alphabetized lines
That you are more than just giving in
This one is for you
For when you were told you were broken
That you needed to be saved
That has not left your mind, sometimes you still believe you
need to be saved
For when you told yourself you were going to hell
Because of who you knew you were
Because of who you could be
Because of who you were afraid not to be

This is for you

The third line
*This one didn't cut straight; the knife left a serrated
footprint*
You bounced between worlds
Yours/theirs/yours/theirs
And it felt like they could never combine into a whole
You resolved to hold your tongue
You tried to make up for all the hurt you left behind at
home
This was a second chance, boarding school,
With people like you, *the special ones*, that's what they
told me
A school of science and math in the bull city
A place where you could hide and untangle
But then have to stuff the creases back together again
when someone looked
You found ways to hastily seal the cracks from the acid
rain
This third line goes way back
You loved deeply back then
You did and you still love them
But you did not love yourself
Even when you wanted to ram your car into the light pole
And told the woman you trusted that things weren't okay
*And went home and watched Gone with the Wind with your
mother*

And no one talked about what had happened
No don't talk about it not even during the first therapy
session
Where you don't understand what's really going on
Why is this therapist so fixated on you and your mother?
This is frightening, isn't it darling
This one is for you

The fourth line
This one is still bleeding
It cut much deeper than the rest
You can see the muscle and bone through spurts of
blood
The pain is liberating
The infections sobering
The throbbing comforting
The number has grown too big to be held comfortably
in any part of your mind
The guilt paints your body triumphantly
In pale colors that reveal the worn parts of you
The ones you gave and the ones that were taken
The ones you can't get back
This one is for you

Read this when it is tempting to cross over the side of
the barricade
When you feel more at home on the unseen side of the
veil

Read this and remember, *this is you saying that you are
beautiful*
Remember that the things you do, they are for you
This is for you

reparations for lost children

I knock on the door. You turn the knob, your tiny hands slipping on the cold metal of the doorknob. I ask if I can come in, you don't say a word but your pupils dilate, evidence that your body's defense mechanism is telling you safety isn't certain. I don't budge, but I soften my voice. I tell you that I just want to see what you're doing, to see what you are playing, if I can just come watch for a moment. Your brow furrows, a developing mind struggling to reason through the complexity of extending trust. Words mean enough to you at this point in your life because you take a step back and open the door enough for me to come in. I step through the doorway and enter your secret room, the one where only you are allowed to come in. The floor is full of scattered things, but organized things, things in deliberate groups and rows. Your imagination: a kingdom untainted by the necrotic touch of disdain, of rejection, of surprise. Your imagination is a world purely erected from the things that bring you joy. The flags grouped by countries allied to one another in your rewritten world, the world of which you drew maps with different colored pens, labeling new borders and old cities and redesigning places where you've never been. These maps sit on the desk for easy reference, to check to see if you're remembering that border correctly (*don't doubt yourself—you have committed this to memory*). The plastic animals and figurines cluster around the flags, groups conglomerated not by politics but by similarities understood simply in juvenile naivety. Their names are ones you find beautiful, feminine and French in origin (*Corinne, Aurélie, Hélène*) but this you'd never say aloud. The dolls have brushed hair and their skirts are pressed. You sing melodies in your head while you play. This I heard while I waited outside the door. All your books are stacked in the corner, alphabetical by author, just in front of where the stuffed animals stand guarding your bed. These are your companions at night, when the darkness threatens to erase everything you love around you, when you don't feel safe and feel scared of all the spaces around you.

But back to this moment. Your face is reddening, embarrassed that I'm seeing the piles of hand-drawn maps and neatly-bulleted lists and the toys and flags scattered in careful piles across the floor. My heart is suddenly heavy, a weight wavering in a limp sling that's threatening to fall down from where it's suspended in midair. I crouch down, looking you straight in the eye, and I tell you that this is beautiful, this is special, that I love how you play. I love the things that your mind interweaves and creates and the things upon which it fixates. I tell you it's okay, there's no need to put things away, to hide them in shame of being seen. There is nothing to be ashamed of, there is nothing to hide. I see the bastille you build against the rumors of an impending revolution, to hide yourself from growing up and seeing how the world rejects the things that you find beautiful. I look you in the eyes as you start to cry. No one ever told you that this was okay, that you didn't have to change or hide or pretend that this would fade away, one day, a phase that would pass as childhood passed. Yes, you are soft, but you are hardened now as I look at my child self and see the parts of myself that are still locked away in their prison cells, deep down in the parts of me that I still haven't unlocked. There is no reason to feel ashamed, I say and I hear myself say fifteen years too late. But now I say it to myself and that spares something from being lost today. I step back, wave goodbye and tell you that I'll come back by again later, shut the door and turn away before the tears start to fall. A rupture tears its way through my ribs and heart and core and my blood spills out in front of me, I see that it is not dirtied like I'd feared as a child but it is crimson, shining and stark and pure. I fall down hard on the cold stone floor but there is a peace in the thud, a relief in knowing that the barricade wasn't breached, that the parts I love most are still safe and still there.

dans l'amour

ah, hope was fragile

surprise, I'm here to save myself

yes, I am enough

Heart strings are finite

Each only goes for so long

Me, you, and the hurt

Can you hear the wind

Tear between the hardened trunks

Of trees with new leaves

he lays his hand down

the touch, the forgiving, the knowing

that I am enough

see the wedding band

a proclamation of hope

me, you, and a cure

for when I yearn to

implode and admit defeat

repeat: I'm enough

17 april 2017

I waited to write down my thoughts until this
morning, hoping that I would be able to more
succinctly describe all that I felt during my
appointment with Bernie yesterday. We did EMDR
based around the need to constantly prove myself to
my environment, the feeling of having been the cause
of people's pain when I can tell something is wrong
with a friend, and of constantly feeling inadequate and
ill-equipped to be in medical school.

These were heavy feelings to sit with, but my eyes
found the rhythm of the movements more naturally
yesterday than they have previously. We made it to
the point where we were focusing on my visceral
response to the session, namely, the tension headache I
tend to get. I was able to visualize it as a thick, chalky
rubber band being stretch through the center of my
head. I saw myself straining to keep it taught, fearing
the repercussions of letting it go, and feeling the
surmounting exhaustion of having to pull against my
own strength continuously.

I realized that the sting of the snap, when the rubber
band finally wrenches itself free from my grip, that
sting of pain is the "hit" of feeling alive that I've been

craving, addictively. I've felt as if I've been in a haze, a dazed fog, without the little moments where pain or excessive stimulation help jolt me into a sensation of presence that I don't seem to have otherwise.

what i learned in medicine: year 1 (may 2017)

I told myself: *I will get better.* After I passed out on the toilet, I told myself: *I will get better.* After I was electrocuted at the fence in the middle of the woods, I told myself: *I will get better.* When my blood ran in rivers against the gradients it was meant to follow, I told myself: *I will get better.* After my panic attack during interview day at UNC SOM, I told myself: *I will get better.*

When I attended Lake Weekend after a friend's funeral, and after a summer of rocky sobriety, I told myself: *I will get better.*

Every night, when I fell asleep to an inner chorus demanding validating credentials for this life I've chosen, I told myself: *I will get better.*

Remember the many days during small group, when I would find myself at school without the ability to speak, that damn disease won you see, that's when I thought to myself, *you will get better.*

I recognized the distance between "I" and "you". That was a hard disparity to reconcile; it's one for which reparations are still incomplete.

It's how I consoled myself, how I supported myself through the minutes and hours when mortality was a concept as real as passing the final exam in our current block.

Hello, my name is Austin, and I am a recovering addict. An addict without a specific Achilles' heel; many things have filtered in and out of the role of a con artist á la savior. The idea of "a hit" was not discriminatory, not for me, I was flexible. I was silent, I was hurt, and I wanted to help usurp the imbalance I struggled against.

I am not perfect. I told myself that I was not enough, that I needed to get better in order to be the person I demanded to be in medical school. To be that "future doctor," the ideology that I believed would save me from something much larger than myself.

I'm thankful that this realization occurred in my first year.

A brief aside: **I am proud of myself**.

But there are moments in which I fear I'm becoming a cliché: *you have to take care of yourself before you can care for someone else.*

For much of the past few years, I did not understand what that meant. I did not understand love for the human condition. I did not understand what it meant to be "me": I'd condemned that part of me that didn't conform, that part that truly loved the people that hurt, the people that society had turned its back against. I understood judgment, and expectations to erect a demigod, not for someone in our world. In short, when I arrived at orientation, I did not understand what I'd signed up for.

I first saw myself as a patient when we discussed someone with an addiction. How do you c0unsel them, why do you preach to them, do you even understand them when you can barely reconcile this within yourself? How dare you look down upon them, how do you judge them, how do you reduce them because you, as a physician-to-be, know so much more about how to be a human?

I felt so small and so large at the same time. It almost tore me apart.

—This was when we finished the Cardiovascular Block, when I was able to leave for a few weeks and I was able to probe around inside me for the jarring pieces that would not stop sparking fires—

I returned to school with a false understanding of what I should be: someone who was able to understand all their tragedies, all their melodramas, all their unresolved hurt, and all of the physical hurt that was incapacitating. This was unreal, for any human. We are not meant to omnisciently carry so much at once.

When I shared a piece of me in *Healer's Art*, I thought that was sufficient liberation. To give a piece of me to strangers, to speak in vague soliloquys, to speak to myself in front of an audience. But it wasn't. Somehow, I failed myself, yet again.

How can I love and serve the best interest of another human being when I couldn't serve the best interest of myself?

That's the question I dealt with. The one I fell to, the one that haunted me, the one that whispered over my shoulder *you have made a mistake. You do not belong here, you aren't like the others. You are too different. You cannot fit in. You cannot do any good. You are too jaded, too ruined, too hurt, too ravaged, too bitter. There is nothing left in you that is worthy of this life.*

That message was easily internalized, for it has lived within a crevice in my chest from the start.

Then the cascade appeared, prominent and relentless. Failed test. Failed sobriety. Failed chastity, failed remission. Failed this, failed that. This is narrative that I've fed myself thus far in our Foundation Phase. What kind of foundation has that set?

I've drawn in permanent ink on myself, to make amends with forces and events that I felt were oppressive, suppressive, demeaning. These things are in my skin, now, they are with me and I cannot look past them. This is what I've learned in medicine: I am not invincible, I am not a demigod, I am not more than I am. But that is okay. That is more than okay.

In medicine, I will have access to a realm of special knowledge with the potential power of healing and with the privilege of understanding the most intimate physical events in a human life. But that realization was something I didn't expect to be immediately self-reflective, to be something that almost killed me, to be something that made me commit to life more strongly than I have ever done before.

This may have been an exercise in self-resolution, but I promise there is a point. Was this an expose, a way to vent things to people whom I don't believe I was able to reach? Was this an extension to those to whom I was afraid to open up, to extend an ounce of faith? But what was the prompt, even, how did I end up at this thought?

What did I learn in medicine, at this point?

I am enough.

I am enough.

I may get better. I will get better. But that is not a requirement for validation.

As I am now, I am enough. *I am enough.*

the loose ends became knots (28 august 2017)

Bernie: Sometimes when we have had violence or pain afflicted upon us, it is empowering to say exactly what was done to us.

He's right. This is what I have needed—to feel justified, to feel able, to claim ownership over the truth—

Me: I was raped.

acknowledgments

I want to thank everyone who contributed to this project as I could not have done it alone. In particular, I want to thank those who have and continue to love and support me unwaveringly.

A few specific thank you's:

Sophie, for being the friend who will always get up from bed to take me to the emergency room;

Shannon, for saving me when we met in the West End and for bringing me endless joy across state lines and continents (as well as your editorial finesse);

Meredith, for listening and understanding me when I've lacked words to speak and for the best playlists a boy could dream of;

Bernie, for the hard, challenging, healing work you have guided me through, and for space where I finally told my entire, uncensored story for the first time;

Jean, for being the first to suggest that my story was worth publication;

My family, for the love you have given me and the work we have both put in to repair things collaterally damaged over the past few years;

and to Paul, pour tout. Vous avez vu quelque chose de beau et sans tache en moi quand je ne pouvais pas le voir. Je vous aimerai jusqu'à la fin.

Enfin, ceci est pour moi-même.

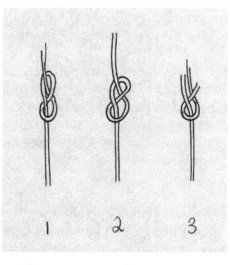

CPSIA information can be obtained
at www.ICGtesting.com
Printed in the USA
LVHW041921230719
625023LV00002B/359/P

9 781618 460486